STUDIES IN ENGLISH LITERATURE

Volume XXX

HENRY FIELDING
AND THE DRY MOCK

A Study of the Techniques of Irony
in His Early Works

by

GEORGE R. LEVINE

State University of New York

1967

MOUTON & CO.

THE HAGUE • PARIS

Printed in The Netherlands by Mouton & Co., Printers, The Hague.

For Joan

PREFACE

The purpose of this study is to examine in detail an aspect of the comic method of one of the great literary craftsmen of the 18th century. I realize, of course, the risks inherent in any attempt to analyze comedy and particularly irony, which George Puttenham in 1589 so aptly characterized as "the drye Mock", but I hope at the same time that I have been able to avoid the fate that E. B. White has predicted is the inevitable consequence of any such analysis: "Humour can be dissected, as a frog can, but the thing dies in the process and the innards are discouraging to any but the pure scientific mind." My hope is that this study will enhance rather than deaden the pleasure in reading Fielding.

Since I consider *Joseph Andrews* to be the culmination of Fielding's early development as an ironist, I have limited this study to those works written between January, 1728 ("The Masquerade") and August, 1742 (the second edition of *Joseph Andrews*). I have included *Jonathan Wild* because it seems to me to have been written largely before *Joseph Andrews*. I have not discussed *Shamela* only because it is a work of almost pure sustained parody containing very little irony. And although I have considered Fielding's miscellaneous works published during this period in my analysis of his ironic techniques, I have limited my illustrations to the plays, *The Champion, Joseph Andrews,* and *Jonathan Wild*.

Although I realize the ultimate impossibility of separating Fielding the ironist from Fielding the playwright-journalist-novelist, my focus has been on the techniques rather than on whole works. I have made an exception of *Joseph Andrews* both because I felt there was a need to show how the techniques of verbal irony functioned collectively in a single work, and because *Joseph Andrews* represents the culmination of Fielding's early development as an ironist.

I wish to thank the graduate school of Columbia University for the grant of a University Fellowship which enabled me to complete much of my preliminary research. I wish also to thank the Committee on Publications and the Committee on the Allocation of Research Funds of the State University of New York for grants that have made possible the publication of this book.

For their kind and always judicious criticism of the early versions of this book, I am grateful to Professors Howard Schless, John H. Middendorf, and especially James L. Clifford, whose love and knowledge of the 18th century has inspired a generation of graduate students at Columbia. For their advice on later versions, I wish to thank Professors Wallace W. Douglas, Joseph I. Fradin, and especially Herbert N. Schneidau, whose perceptive criticism has helped me in more ways than I can possibly acknowledge here.

For permission to reprint a section of Chapter II that originally appeared (in somewhat different form) under the title, "Henry Fielding's 'Defense' of the Stage Licensing Act", I am grateful to the editors of *English Language Notes* (Vol. II, March, 1965).

State University of New York at Buffalo
July, 1965   G. R. L.

CONTENTS

I

IRONY IN THE 18TH CENTURY

As a novelist, Henry Fielding was remarkably inventive in many ways, but as an ironist he was quite conventional. The specific techniques that he employed during his early years as a writer conform fairly closely to those that his contemporaries were using consciously as well as to many that were simply implicit in the different contextual meanings of the word *irony*. Several of these techniques had, of course, been associated with *irony* since the time of Socrates, but many more had crept imperceptibly into use in succeeding ages.[1] To see Fielding's irony within this historic context, it is important that we have some understanding of the techniques that his contemporaries associated with rhetorical irony.[2] For this, however, we must rely on our knowledge of the ways in which people defined the word in their dictionaries and rhetorics and, more important, of the ways in which they used it in literary contexts, for although 18th century writers employed irony extensively and discussed it frequently, and although references to the word *irony* as a general rhetorical device turn up quite often in the 18th century, few writers consciously took the trouble

---

[1] For a detailed discussion of the history of irony from the Greeks through the mid-eighteenth century, see G. G. Sedgewick, *Of Irony, Especially in Drama* (Toronto, 1948), chapter I; J. A. K. Thomson, *Irony, An Historical Introduction* (London, 1926); and Norman Knox, *The Word Irony and its Context, 1500-1755* (Durham, North Carolina, 1961), chapter I.

[2] Dramatic irony was employed by many writers, including Fielding, but there is little evidence to indicate that many people were ever consciously aware of it *as* irony, for it was seldom discussed during or prior to the 18th century. See Knox, pp. 92-8 and 186.

to differentiate carefully between the concept and the mode, or between the different techniques themselves.[3]

A. IRONY AND SATIRE IN THE 18TH CENTURY

The history of the word *irony* in the 18th century [4] is characterized both by the blurring of distinctions established by the conventional definitions of the term, and by the degree to which *irony* came to be synonymous with *satire*. When defining the term, writers invariably quoted the definitions that could be found in any one of the standard dictionaries or rhetorics, but their use of the term in context suggests that – consciously or not – they gave to *irony* a great variety of meanings, some of which were quite far removed from the actual definitions,[5] but most of which were related in some way to satire.

The contextual meanings of *irony* naturally included the stock definitions: it could refer to a mode of stating something either opposite to or different from what is really meant; it could refer to blame-by-praise, or praise-by-blame, or, finally, to any kind of mockery or scoffing.[6] But the many more contextual meanings had often only the most tenuous association with the term. Thus, *irony* was equated with such things as "ambiguous language intended to conceal part of its meaning from part of the audience",[7] or "any kind of contrary expression",[8] or simply "any discourse not meant to be taken seriously".[9]

---

[3] See Knox, pp. 7-16, 24-30. Actually, it was not until well into the following century that an English critic consciously attempted to distinguish between the concept and the specific techniques through which the ironist achieves his effects. See Sedgewick, p. 19. The work referred to was Bishop Connop Thirlwall's essay, "On the Irony of Sophocles", *Philological Museum*, II (1833), pp. 483-537.

[4] For the history of the word *irony* in the 18th century, I am indebted to Mr. Knox's valuable study (see note 1 above). I have followed Mr. Knox in not attempting to consider the use of *irony* beyond 1755.

[5] Knox, chapter II.

[6] *Ibid.*, pp. 30-4.

[7] *Ibid.*, pp. 43-4.

[8] *Ibid.*, pp. 77-8.

[9] *Ibid.*, p. 90.

What is particularly significant here is the degree of correlation between contextual usage and technique. Inadvertently, through their use of the word, writers were distinguishing between the various techniques of irony. Indeed, in his illuminating study, Norman Knox has shown that *irony* was employed in no less than ten different ways, ranging from "pretense and deception" to "dramatic irony",[10] and most of these reflect specific ironic techniques. The most striking feature of Mr. Knox's categories is the way in which the satiric function has intruded itself into his discussions of most of these meanings. There are, in fact, only three that serve other purposes – praise-by-blame, the relatively minor "Irony as any discourse not meant to be taken seriously", and "dramatic irony". Significantly, the most popular meaning of *irony* in the first half of the 18th century was blame-by-praise, and this coincides with one of the conventional dictionary definitions.[11] The other meanings of *irony*, however, tend to lead it farther and farther away from the conventional definitions, and writers began to identify as ironic many things that were not even closely related to the term as consciously defined.[12] This was in all proba-

---

[10]   I. *Irony* as pretense and deception: A. Constant dissimulation, B. Self-depreciation in order to achieve a practical end, C. falsely attributing some attitude or act to another;
II. *Irony* as limited deception: A. a temporary deception which tricks one's interlocutor into revealing the truth, B. ambiguous language intended to conceal part of its meaning from part of the audience;
III. *Irony* as blame-by-praise and praise-by-blame: A. Irony of manner, B. limited discourse (1) praise-by-blame, (2) blame-by-praise;
IV. *Irony* as saying the contrary of what one means for emphasis, the contrary being neither false praise nor false blame: A. By pretending to omit what one is all the while asserting, B. by using any kind of contrary expression;
V. *Irony* as understatement: A. Denial of the contrary, B. Intimation;
VI. *Irony* as indirection: A. statement of a corollary of one's criticism without statement of the criticism itself, B. meaningful reply to a submerged meaning of a remark;
VII. *Irony* as the grave elaboration of a fiction for the purpose of casual satire or aimless mystification;
VIII. *Irony* as any discourse not meant to be taken seriously;
IX. *Irony* as any kind of derisive attack;
X. Dramatic irony (Knox, pp. 38-98).
[11]   Knox, p. 12.
[12]   *Ibid.*, p. 14.

bility a result of the transference to *irony* of the many terms that were accurately and inaccurately associated with satire. More specifically, it may well have been the result of confusion about such related terms as *raillery, burlesque,* and *banter,* which were frequently used interchangeably.[13] In Anthony Collins' *Discourse Concerning Ridicule and Irony in Writing,* for example, *drollery* is used almost without exception as a synonym for *irony.*[14] An extreme in this gradual obfuscation of the term seems to have been reached when *irony* came to be considered synonymous with "any kind of satiric attack".[15]

These contextual meanings of *irony* are valuable for the insight they give us into how the literary predilections of the time influenced the use which writers made of the word, as well as for what they tell us about the techniques that had gained currency. This process was certainly not a conscious one, for contextual meanings frequently reflect more about a writer's literary milieu than he is usually aware of.[16] Occasionally, however, writers did associate quite explicitly the techniques of irony with satire. Charles Jarvis, for example, in the preface to his 1742 translation of Cervantes' *Don Quixote,* noted that "the ironical is the most agreeable and perhaps the strongest of all kinds of satire".[17] And Anthony Collins in his *Discourse* equated "Men of Irony" with "Droles and Satirists".[18]

However much we may theorize and speculate about the causes for the semantic intrusion of one term upon another, the one cause

---

[13]   *Ibid.,* pp. 189-90.

[14]   Anthony Collins, *A Discourse Concerning Ridicule and Irony in Writing* (London, 1729), p. 30. See also pp. 10, 17, 18, 25, 39, 50, 52, 56, 62, and 64.

[15]   *Ibid.,* p. 90.

[16]   This same process seems to be going on today with the word *irony.* Although the OED defines it one way, the use to which Cleanth Brooks and Northrop Frye put *irony* reflects their concern with critical tendencies of the twentieth century. It seems improbable that an eighteenth-century writer would ever have used *irony* to mean something which modifies the tone or texture of a poem; nor, on the other hand, does it seem probable that Cleanth Brooks today would use *irony* as a word descriptive of any kind of satiric device.

[17]   Charles Jarvis, Preface to *Don Quixote* (London, 1742), pp. vi-vii.

[18]   Collins, p. 30.

that we can point to with certainty is the impact of Swift on his age. To Swift belongs the major credit for fostering an interest in irony as a mode of satire in the 18th century, for no other writer of this period used irony so effectively. The *Tale of a Tub,* for example, is a masterpiece of ironic manipulation of the reader in which irony is piled high upon irony. The reader is forced to approach this work as he would an area where he suspects quicksand – but may find flypaper; he never knows when he might take an imprudent step – and get stuck. Not surprisingly, tributes from his admirers often praised him specifically for his skill as an ironist. Anthony Collins referred to Swift in 1729 as "one of the greatest Droles [i.e., ironists] that ever appeared".[19] And in 1739, the English translation of Dedekind's *Grobianus* was dedicated to Swift, "who first introduc'd into these Kingdoms . . . an Ironical Manner of Writing".[20] Even an anonymous and otherwise antagonistic Whig pamphleteer, in *An Essay Upon the Taste and Writings of the Present Times*, admitted that Swift was the unequalled "Tyrant" of ridicule:

But of all those Tyrants that have, in any Age or Nation, made themselves dreadful by any of the various Parts of Ridicule, there was perhaps never one that equall'd in Power our most facetious Countryman Dr. *Swift*. For by this one single Talent he has reign'd absolute in the witty World for upwards of thirty years. – He has open'd a Vein of Humour, which in the most humourous Nation of the World was never heard of before.[21]

Swift's ironic boast in "Verses on the Death of Dr. Swift, 1731", then, was not too far from the truth:

> Arbuthnot is no more my friend,
> Who dares to Irony pretend,
> Which I was born to introduce,
> Refin'd it first, and shew'd its use (ll. 55-8) [22]

---

[19] *Ibid.*, p. 39.
[20] Friedrich Dedekind, *Grobianus; or the Complete Booby: An Ironical Poem*, translated by Roger Bull (London, 1739),
[21] [Anon.], *An Essay Upon the Taste and Writings of the Present Times* (London, 1728), pp. 5-6. Cited in Knox, pp. 182-3.
[22] Jonathan Swift, *Poems*, ed. Harold Williams (London, 1958), II, p. 555.

Yet in a letter to Bathurst a few months before, he was being perhaps unduly modest when he said: "I pretend to have been an
improver on the subjects of satire and praise. . . ." [23] The truth of
the matter probably lies between the ironic boast and the humble
admission. Swift did not introduce irony to England, but he was
probably the single most important influence upon its use and
development, let alone its popularity, in the 18th century.

Quite apart from Swift, the obsession with manner and decorum
was one of the major factors in the Augustans' growing commit-
ment to irony and the ironic mode. This would seem to account
for the preference which writers such as Pope, Swift, and Fielding
had for a mode that was both refined and subtle, and that depended for its effects upon a considerable degree of intellectual sophistication. Just as these men distinguished between the Grub-Street
"mob" on the one hand, and the intellectual aristocracy on the
other, so was there a similar contrast in the respective modes of
expression. The coarse, broad humor of "banter", with its lack of
refinement and subtlety, was to the mob what irony, with its sharp
cutting edge, its elegance and sophistication of style, was to those
who harbored the ideal of an intellectual elite,[24] those who considered themselves an "aristocracy of brains", to use David
Worcester's phrase. And to these men, the ironic pose was perfectly in keeping with what Swift himself ironically referred to as
"the Sin of Wit".

This association of banter and the mob is made quite explicitly
again and again throughout the first half of the 18th century. In
the Apology to *A Tale of a Tub*, for example, Swift identifies the
mob as "those who have no share or taste of either [wit], the
noblest and most useful gift of human nature [or of humour], the
most agreeable". These men are "insensible" to wit and humour,
Swift continues, and "by their pride, pedantry, and ill manners,

---

[23]   *The Correspondence of Jonathan Swift*, ed. F. Elrington Ball (London,
1913), IV, p. 166.
[24]   This association of mob and banter was first brought to my attention
by Ian Watt, "The Ironic Tradition in Augustan Prose from Swift to
Johnson", in *Restoration and Augustan Prose* (Los Angeles, 1956), pp.
20-4.

lay themselves bare to the lashes of both . . .". Then, in defending the *Tale* against the charge of banter, he asks, "But if this bantering, as they call it, be so despisable a thing, whence comes it to pass that they have such a perpetual itch toward it themselves?" [25]

Shaftesbury, in his discussion of "Character" in *The Regimen*, reflects a similar awareness of the contrast between the two modes of expression – the genteel, highly-polished irony, and "controversy", which is synonymous, as Shaftesbury uses it, to "banter". It is to the ironic manner of a Socrates – characterized by "grace and accommodation" – that he insists we must ultimately turn when confronted with the difficulties of existing in a "rotten" society that delights only in ephemeral pleasures and buffoonery.[26]

Lord Chesterfield demonstrates the same repugnance to "audible laughter", a specific type of buffoonery, which he also associates quite explicitly with the mob. In warning his son against any displays of merriment, he says:

> Having mentioned laughing, I must particularly warn you against it: and I could heartily wish that you may often be seen to smile, but never heard to laugh while you live. Frequent and loud laughter is the characteristic of folly and ill manners: it is the manner in which the mob express their silly joy at silly things: and they call it being merry. In my mind there is nothing so illiberal and so ill-bred, as audible laughter. . . .[27]

Anthony Collins, in his *Discourse*, makes a further distinction between "polite" and "gross" modes of irony – the latter clearly comparable to what Swift meant by "banter".

> Tho I have endeavoured to defend the Use of *Ridicule* and *Irony*, yet it is such *Irony* and *Ridicule* only as is fit for polite Persons to use. As to the gross *Irony* and *Ridicule*, I disapprove of it, as I do other Faults in Writing.[28]

---

[25] Jonathan Swift, *A Tale of a Tub*, ed. A. C. Guthkelch and D. Nichol Smith (Oxford, 1920), pp. 18-19.
[26] Anthony Ashley Cooper, Earl of Shaftesbury, *Life, Unpublished Letters and Philosophical Regimen*, ed. Benjamin Rand (New York, 1900), p. 192.
[27] *The Letters of Lord Chesterfield*, ed. Bonamy Dobrée (London, 1932), III, pp. 1115-1116 (March 9, 1748).
[28] Collins, p. 77.

In Fielding we find reflected these same attitudes toward the mob and its crude and corrupt manner. He treats it, in fact, as the most contemptible segment of society. In *Tom Jones*, so intent is he that his reader not mistake his use of the word *mob*, that he adds a rare footnote to his text: "Wherever this word occurs in our writings, it intends persons without virtue or sense, in all stations; and many of the highest rank are often meant by it" (I, ix). And later, in several issues of the *Covent-Garden Journal*, he attacks both the mob (the epigraph for No. 49, for example, is Horace's *"Odi Profanum vulgus"*, which Fielding translates as *"I hate the mob"* [29]) and its manner, which in this case is specifically an incapacity for clear expression:

The Part which this fourth Estate [i.e., the mob] seems antiently to have claimed was to watch over and controll the other three [Kings, Lords, Commons]. This indeed they have seldom asserted in plain Words, which is possibly the principal Reason why our Historians have never explicitly assigned them their Share of Power in the Constitution, tho' this Estate have so often exercised it, and so clearly asserted their Right to it by Force of Arms; to wit, by Fists, Staves, Knives, Clubs, Scythes, and other such offensive Weapons. [30]

In the earlier "Essay on Conversation", however, he makes explicit his adherence to the same kind of distinction made by Anthony Collins, that between harsh raillery (the manner of the mob) and gentle raillery (the manner of those of "good breeding"). As is clear from his subsequent use of the term, *raillery* here is intended to be synonymous with *irony*.

But I must not dismiss this subject without some animadversions on a particular species of pleasantry, which, though I am far from being desirous of banishing from conversation, requires, most certainly, some reins to govern, and some rule to direct it. The reader may perhaps guess, I mean Raillery; to which I may apply the Fable of the lap-dog and the ass; for while in some hands it diverts and delights us with its dexterity and gentleness, in others, it paws, daubs, offends and hurts. [31]

[29] *The Covent-Garden Journal*, ed. Gerard E. Jensen (New Haven, 1915), II, p. 31.
[30] *Ibid.*, p. 23.
[31] *The Complete Works of Henry Fielding*, ed. W. E. Henley (New York, 1902), XIV, p. 274.

Later, in the same essay, he discusses at greater length the incompatibility of gentle and harsh raillery:

> The raillery which is consistent with good-breeding, is a gentle animadversion on some foible; which, while it raises a laugh in the rest of the company, doth not put the person rallied out of countenance, or expose him to shame and contempt. On the contrary, the jest should be so delicate, that the object of it should be capable of joining in the mirth it occasions.[32]

However appealing the manner of the ironist and however effective the mode, the one major reservation these writers had about irony was the possibility that irony was potentially self-defeating, for it had to be just obvious enough not to be missed, yet subtle enough to take in the unsuspecting reader.[33] This is, of course, a problem that has always confronted the ironist. If he is too subtle, his irony may be detected not at all or too late to be effective. As with good acting – and the ironist is very much the actor playing a self-conscious role – good timing is crucial to the success of the performance. Defoe's *The Shortest Way With the Dissenters* is an excellent example of poor timing (rather than of irony that was "too successful" – as some critics have insisted), for it was not until some weeks after it was published that both dissenters and Anglicans realized whose side Defoe was really on. Although such subtlety as Defoe employed may have enhanced the ultimate literary value of his irony, its immediate rhetorical value was lost. Indeed, in Defoe's case not only was the point of the pamphlet missed but his argument was even turned against him.[34]

On the other hand, the ironist cannot make his meaning too apparent, for the irony would then be wasted. This is probably what detracts from the effectiveness of sarcasm, which, properly

---

[32] *Ibid.*, p. 275.
[33] Mr. Knox discusses this problem in considerable detail. See pp. 146-62.
[34] Bonamy Dobrée goes so far as to suggest that *The Shortest Way* was not ironic at all because of Defoe's failure to "push the matter discussed over the edge of the plausible; it is, indeed, an admirable but faithful copy of what the high-flyers were urging" (*English Literature in the Early 18th Century*, New York, 1959, p. 46). Cf. John H. Ross, *Swift and Defoe: A Study in Relationship* (Berkeley, 1941), pp. 81-5 for an earlier statement of this idea.

speaking, must be considered a mode of irony, but which, in fact, is so transparent a form of pretense as to make it virtually useless as a literary device. The most effective form of irony depends upon the neat – but deadly – rapier thrust rather than the brutal "flesh-tearing" of sarcasm. The ironist's real problem, then – of major concern to 18th century critics – is that he must constantly seek the mean between the two extremes, a mean which J. A. K. Thomson has aptly described as the "trembling equipoise between jest and earnest".[35]

B. THE TECHNIQUES OF IRONY IN THE 18TH CENTURY

The specific techniques which Fielding's contemporaries were using during the first half of the 18th century fall into two distinct categories: those which are implicit in the contextual meanings of the word *irony*, and those which modern critics have derived directly from an examination of the methods of the major ironists. Although these two categories are mutually inclusive, the second is, as we might expect, considerably broader in scope than the first, since a concern (sometimes, unfortunately, an obsession) for ironic subtleties has been one of the legacies of the New Criticism.

There are several techniques associated with blame-by-praise, the dominant contextual meaning of the word *irony* in the first half of the 18th century.[36] The most popular was direct praise – a simple reversal of statement or word. Other techniques included a variety of increasingly elaborate poses, from pretended innocence or humility (which Mr. Knox has called Socratic self-depreciation) to the mask or *persona*, the fictitious "author" who either embodied directly or suggested innocently all of the things the ironist was attacking.

The less elaborate poses among the blame-by-praise techniques included the ironic concession, where the ironist falsely conceded the validity of a statement; ironic advice, where the ironist offered

[35] Thomson, *Irony*, p. 166.
[36] See Knox, pp. 99-140.

false advice which somehow managed to embody some form of elaborate praise; and the ironic defense, where the ironist defended an absurd premise by extending it to an even more absurd conclusion. Closely related to this technique was the fallacious argument, which involved either the attribution of false motives to an action or the use of a false enthymeme.[37]

The most clearly defined of those techniques implicit in the contextual meanings of *irony* that were not associated with blame-by-praise were praise-by-blame; the two forms of understatement, the conventional rhetorical method involving either diminution (as in, "Yes, Swift was something of a satirist") and denial of the contrary (as in, "Swift was no mean satirist"); and the use of a contrary statement for emphasis (rather than blame).[38] Although understatement could be and was used as a satiric technique, these techniques were generally more strictly comic than satiric in purpose. They were, more properly, a function of style.

Of the ironic techniques which modern textual critics have isolated, the *persona* or ironic mask has been by far the most popular and has received the most critical attention in recent years. Despite the many distortions of meaning which, as Irwin Ehrenpreis has pointed out,[39] *persona*-hunting has engendered, it cannot be denied that the ironic mask was a major device in the hands of such consummate ironists as Pope and Swift.[40] Indeed, so thorough-

---

[37] Although burlesque is quite distinct as a satiric technique in the early 18th century, it did appear frequently as one of the contextual meanings of *irony* as blame-by-praise. I have not included it in this description of the blame-by-praise techniques only because most of the other techniques do eventually shade off into burlesque if pushed far enough (Knox, p. 126). The difference between burlesque and ironic concession, for example, is really one of degree rather than of substance.

[38] Knox, pp. 55-8, 78-82, and 76-78.

[39] Irwin Ehrenpreis, "Personae", *Restoration and 18th Century Literature: Essays in Honor of A. D. McKillop* (Chicago, 1963), pp. 25-37.

[40] See, for example, William B. Ewald, *The Masks of Jonathan Swift* (Cambridge, 1954); Maynard Mack, "The Muse of Satire", *Yale Review*, XLI (1951), pp. 80-92; Rebecca Price Parkin, *The Poetic Workmanship of Alexander Pope* (Minneapolis, 1955), chapter II; John M. Bullitt, *Jonathan Swift and the Anatomy of Satire* (Cambridge, 1953), chapter II; Martin Price, *Swift's Rhetorical Art* (New Haven, 1953), chapter IV; Ian Watt, "The Ironic Tradition", pp. 19-46; Thomas R. Edwards, Jr., *This Dark Estate: A Reading of Pope* (Berkeley, 1963), chapter IV.

ly does the ironic mask inform such satires as *Gulliver's Travels*
and "A Modest Proposal" that it has become almost impossible
to discuss the irony of these works without granting some attention to Swift's *personae.*

Of comparable subtlety is a technique that Reuben Brower has
called "allusive irony". Specific allusions to people, ideas, situations, literary conventions, etc. outside the immediate framework
of the work clash discordantly with the specific objects of the
irony within the work. Dryden's ironic praise of Corah in "Ab-
salom and Achitophel" is particularly rich in allusions of this type
and demonstrates the extraordinary sophistication of this technique:

> Yet, Corah, thou shalt from oblivion pass:
> Erect thyself, thou monumental brass,
> High as the serpent of thy metal made,
> While nations stand secure beneath thy shade. (ll. 632-635)

The discordant allusions are to be found mainly in Dryden's use
of "monumental brass", in which, as Mr. Brower shows, the high
Latinate connotations of "monumental" clash with what is also a
parody of Horace's "Exegi monumentum aere perennius . . .".
And the ecclesiastical connotations of "brass" monuments in an
English church clash with "brass" as "monumental" effrontery.[41]

An aspect of allusive irony is a device that Swift employed
often – connotative ambivalence, the simultaneous presence of
incompatible but relevant connotations. In describing this technique – which he calls "redefinition" – Martin Price goes so far
as to call this "the principal method of irony".[42] The irony here
stems from the "simultaneous presentation of the 'official version' and the 'real meaning' in the same term".[43] Thus, the irony
of "merits" in a section of Swift's letter to the October Club stems
from the conflict of two relevant meanings, "its party sense of

---

[41]   Reuben Brower, *Alexander Pope: The Poetry of Allusion* (Oxford,
1959), pp. 6-8. Pope also employs allusive irony; see Brower, pp. 144 and
267.
[42]   Price, p. 24.
[43]   *Ibid.*, pp. 24-5.

complete subjection to common interest and its usual moral sense of virtuous efforts".[44]

I well remember the Clamours often raised during the Reign of that Party against the Leaders, by those who thought their Merits were not rewarded; and they had Reason on their Side; [this last phrase, according to Mr. Price, was the clue to Swift's irony here] because it is, no doubt, a Misfortune to forfeit *Honour* and *Conscience* for Nothing.[45]

Blame-by-praise and praise-by-blame are, of course, basic techniques that are found throughout the writings of 18th-century ironists.[46] They are the most easily recognizable of the ironic devices, for they usually involved a fairly straightforward inversion of terms: good is bad, bad is good. This is not to suggest, however, that the transparency of the method diminished the effectiveness of the irony. Whatever one may say about the sophistication of Swift's *Vindication of ... Lord C[artere]t* or Fielding's *Jonathan Wild*, much of the ironic impact of both of these works stems from the use of just this technique.

Several of the 18th-century techniques isolated by modern critics [47] are really aspects of dramatic irony, the non-rhetorical technique involving a clash between the degrees of awareness of author and reader, or between actor-character and reader-spectator. Thus, A. E. Dyson, in describing the ironic betrayal of the reader of *Gulliver's Travels*, is in reality concerning himself with just such contrasts of awareness among those readers who "must not only be betrayed but see that [they have] been betrayed".[48] Similar-

[44] *Ibid.*, p. 24.
[45] "Some Advice ... to Members of the October Club", *The Prose Works of Jonathan Swift*, ed. Herbert Davis (Oxford, 1939-62), VI, p. 77.
[46] See Bullitt, pp. 50-6, and Brower, p. 240 for discussions of these techniques in Swift and Pope respectively.
[47] Parkin, chapter III (elegiac irony and both-and irony); A. E. Dyson, "Swift: The Metamorphosis of Irony", *Essays and Studies* (1958), pp. 53-67 (ironic betrayal); Ruby Redinger, "Jonathan Swift, the Disenchanter", *American Scholar*, XV (Spring, 1946), pp. 221-2 (Bickerstaffian irony); and William Empson, "*Tom Jones*", *Kenyon Review*, XX, No. 2 (Spring, 1958), pp. 217-49 (double irony). See also an earlier discussion of double irony in *The Beggar's Opera* in Empson's *Some Versions of Pastoral* (New York, 1960), pp. 200-40.
[48] Dyson, "Swift", pp. 65-6.

ly, Howard L. Koonce's discussion of Defoe's use of irony in *Moll Flanders* [49] focuses on the dramatic ironic tension between the criminal and the moral, and Moll's failure to relate one to the other, even though he uses only the general term *irony* throughout his essay. Mr. Empson's "double irony" in *Tom Jones* is a more complex version of the dramatic-ironic betrayal, for as Mr. Empson sees it, Fielding is really writing to two kinds of readers – one who is never deceived by the irony and the other who is always deceived – or, to use the terms of dramatic irony specifically, one who is always aware and one who is never aware. What the latter reader fails to grasp is Fielding's habit of *appearing* to favor what he is in reality rejecting. What both readers are faced with then, is the almost total unreliability of surface meaning in *Tom Jones*, whose very style, Mr. Empson insists, "is a habitual double irony".[50]

Of particular importance to Swift's irony is the ironic defense, which most frequently took the form of an elaborate and increasingly absurd extension of an ironic premise,[51] as in his *Argument Against Abolishing Christianity*. On many occasions, Swift used the elaborate but false analogy as the vehicle for his ironic defense [52] as well as the false syllogism, in which a proof is made ridiculous by the deliberate ambiguity of its terms, one of which may be taken in its literal sense, the other in its figurative.[53] Thus, in the Introduction to *A Tale of a Tub*, Swift deduces with marvelous illogic a method for "obtaining attention in public":

... Air being a heavy body, and therefore (according to the system of Epicurus) continually descending, must needs be more so, when loaden and pressed down by words; which are also bodies of much weight and gravity, as it is manifest from those deep impressions

[49] "Moll's Muddle: Defoe's Use of Irony in *Moll Flanders*", *English Literary History*, XXX (1963), pp. 377-94.
[50] Empson, "*Tom Jones*", p. 219.
[51] See Bullitt, pp. 97-9. Cf. A. R. Humphreys' "elaborate proof of the blindingly obvious" in "Fielding's Irony: Its Method and Effects", in *Fielding: A Collection of Critical Essays*, ed. R. Paulson (Englewood Cliffs, New Jersey, 1962), pp. 19-21.
[52] F. R. Leavis, "The Irony of Swift", *Scrutiny*, II (1934), pp. 369-70.
[53] Bullitt, pp. 117-18.

they make and leave upon us; and therefore must be delivered from
a due altitude, or else they will neither carry a good aim, nor fall
down with a sufficient force.[54]

Other techniques that modern critics have culled from numerous
18th-century sources – but particularly from Pope and Swift –
are the ironic concession, ironic advice, and understatement [55] –
essentially the same techniques that were implicit in the contextual meanings of *irony* – and, finally, Pope's ironic use of zeugma, or,
as Rebecca Parkin has called it, "the irony of false equation".[56]

What should be immediately apparent is the degree to which
those techniques implicit in the contextual meanings of *irony* support those which modern textual analysis has revealed. Despite
the absence of any extended discussions of ironic techniques *per
se* in the first half of the 18th century, such proof as Mr. Knox's
study affords makes it abundantly clear that these were indeed the
techniques employed by Fielding's contemporaries and immediate
predecessors, and are not merely the product of overzealous
modern textual critics who strain to discover subtleties (including
ironies) beneath every polished facade.

C. FIELDING AND IRONY

Fielding's own techniques, as I shall attempt to show in subsequent
chapters, conformed fairly closely to those I have been describing.
Whatever originality his irony does manifest can be found primarily in his variations on several of the more popular devices, such
as the use of incompatible connotations. His use of the word
irony, however, and his attitude toward the dangers inherent in

[54] Swift, *Tale of a Tub*, p. 60.
[55] Brower, pp. 251 and 309 (for ironic concession and advice); and Bullitt, pp. 44-9 and Brower, p. 245 (for understatement).
[56] Parkin, pp. 45-6; see also Maynard Mack, "Wit and Poetry and Pope:
Some Observations on his Imagery", *Eighteenth Century English Literature*, ed. James L. Clifford (New York, 1959), pp. 30-1; W. K. Wimsatt,
"Rhetoric and Poems: The Example of Pope", *English Institute Essays,
1948* (New York, 1949), pp. 194-6; and Austin Warren, "The Mask of
Pope", *Sewanee Review* (Winter, 1946), pp. 19-33.

the ironic mode were strictly conventional. Whenever the word
appeared in his works, it normally referred to a comic verbal device
which corresponded to one of the blame-by-praise techniques that
were most commonly associated with *irony* in his day.[57] In a note
to his translation of *Plutus* (1742), he uses *irony* to mean blame-
by-praise through fallacious argument.

> *Poverty.* Well then, I proceed now to the Purity of Men's Manners,
> and I shall convince you, that Good-Manners dwell entirely with me;
> for all Abuse belongs to Riches.
>   *Chrom.* O Certainly! for to steal and to break open Houses, is, no
> doubt, a very mannerly thing.
>   *Blepsid.* Yes, by Jove: It must be certainly very reputable *, if the
> Thief be obliged to conceal himself.
>   * ... the Meaning, if it wants Explanation, is, that it must be a very
> reputable Thing indeed, which a Man is obliged to hide himself for having
> done. We need not observe that this is spoke ironically.[58]

And in the Preface to *David Simple,* he uses the term to signify
blame-by-praise through the device of the fictitious character or
persona. He is comparing *David Simple* to comic epics of the past.

> This fable hath in it these three difficult ingredients, which will be
> found on consideration to be always necessary to works of this kind,
> viz., that the main end or scope be at once amiable, ridiculous, and
> natural.
>   If it be said that some of the comic performances I have above
> mentioned differ in the first of these, and set before us the odious
> instead of the amiable; I answer, that is far from being one of their
> perfections; and of this the authors themselves seem so sensible, that
> they endeavour to deceive the reader by false glosses and colours,
> and by the help of irony at least to represent the aim and design of
> their heroes in a favourable and agreeable light.[59]

---

[57]   To present as fully as possible Fielding's attitudes toward *irony*, I have
in this instance considered all of Fielding's writings. The following, however, is not intended to constitute a complete listing of all of Fielding's
uses of the word, but I have attempted to include all of the different
meanings Fielding ever attributed to it.
[58]   *Plutus, the God of Riches, A Comedy. Translated from the Original
Greek of Aristophanes; with Large Notes, Explanatory and Critical*, by
Henry Fielding, Esq. and the Reverend [William] Young (London, 1742),
pp. 55-6.
[59]   Preface to *David Simple, Works* (Henley), XVI, p. 11.

In the *Covent-Garden Journal*, the word appears as blame through direct praise. Fielding is discussing certain biblical references to *wisdom*:

> By Wisdom here, I mean that Wisdom of this World, which St. Paul expressly tells us is *Folly*; that Wisdom *of the Wise*, which, as we read both in Isaiah and in the Corinthians, is threatned with Destruction: Lastly, I here intend that Wisdom in the Abundance of which, as the Preacher tells us, there is *much of Grief*; which, if true, would be alone sufficient to evince the extreme Folly of those who covet and pursue such Wisdom.
>
> But tho' the Scriptures in the Places above cited, and in many others do very severely treat this Character of Worldly or mock Wisdom, they have not, I think, very fully described it, unless perhaps Solomon hath done this ironically under the Name of Folly. An Opinion to which I am much inclined; and indeed what is said in the 10th Chapter of Ecclesiastes of the great Exaltation of a Fool, must be understood of a Fool in Repute, and such is the Wise Man here pointed at.
>
> In the same Manner, the best writers among the Heathens have obscurely and ironically characterized this Wisdom.[60]

There are also several instances in Fielding's works where *irony* assumes some of the more peripheral meanings of satire: in *Joseph Andrews* the word appears to mean nothing more than mockery. In one of the early scenes in the novel, Slipslop indignantly accuses Joseph of being ironic because she thinks that he is mocking her.

> "Sure nothing can be a more simple contract in a woman, than to place her affections on a boy. If I had ever thought it would have been my fate, I should have wished to die a thousand deaths rather than live to see that day. If we like a man, the lightest hint sophisticates. Whereas a boy proposes upon us to break through all regulations of modesty, before we can make any oppression upon him." Joseph, who did not understand a word she said, answered, "Yes, Madam." – "Yes, Madam!" replied Mrs. Slipslop with some warmth, "Do you intend to result my passion? Is it not enough, ungrateful as you are, to make no return to all the favours I have done you; but you must treat me with ironing? Barbarous monster! how have I deserved that my passion should be resulted and treated with ironing?" [61]

60   *The Covent-Garden Journal*, II, p. 126.
61   *Joseph Andrews*, ed. Maynard Mack (New York, 1948), p. 17 (I, vi).

And in *The Covent-Garden Journal,* Fielding uses the word as synonymous with an indirect form of irony which Mr. Knox has called a "statement of a corollary of one's criticism without statement of the criticism itself".

"IT is very remarkable, says M. Dacier, that Horace should attribute all the Miseries of Rome, and all the civil Wars of the Romans to no other Cause than to their Adulteries." And this seems to me the more remarkable when we consider the Character of the Poet who hath given us this Opinion. We have not here the Sentiments of a recluse Pedant, who might be suspected of Ignorance, of a cynic Philosopher, who might be accused of Malice, or of a Christian Divine, whom some would insinuate to be swayed by Interest; but we have before us the Words of a Man of the World, who lived in the politest, and most splendid of Courts, and in the Intimacy of the greatest Men of that Court; of one who united in himself the several Characters of the Gentleman, the Politician, the Moralist, the Scholar, the Poet, the Wit, and the Man of Sense.

Nor is there in these lines the least Appearance of Jest or Irony; on the contrary, they are introduced in one of his gravest Odes, and which was written on the most solemn Occasion; an Ode addressed to his Countrymen, lamenting the wretched Condition into which they were fallen, tracing their political Diseases up to their Source, and pointing out the Methods of their Cure. In this Ode he mentions the Pollutions of the Marriage Bed as the Cause of all the Corruptions of Rome.[62]

Fielding is implying, in other words, that if Horace were being ironic, the "Pollutions of the Marriage Bed" would be the corollary of Horace's real but unstated criticism – the moral degeneracy of the Romans.

In *The Modern Husband, irony* is used as the statement of something contrary to what one means without implying false praise or blame. Gaywit is attempting to tell Emilia that he loves her, but Emilia finds his gravity too much out of character.

Emilia. Nay, this is so extravagant a flight, I know not what to call it.
Mr. Gaywit. Nor I – call it a just admiration of the highest worth, call it the tenderest friendship, if you please; though much I fear it merits the sweetest, softest name that can be given to any of our passions. If there be a passion pure without alloy, as tender and soft,

as violent and strong, you cannot sure miscall it by that name.
Emilia. You grow now too philosophical for me to understand you: besides, you would, I am sure, be best understood ironically; for who can believe anything of Mr. Gaywit, when he hath asserted that he is unhappy? [63]

There is also at least one occasion when Fielding has a character use *irony* as praise-by-blame. In *The Temple Beau*, Young Pedant refuses to allow Lady Lucy Pedant to insult him and turns her derogatory comments directed against him into ironic praise.

L. Lucy. You are a coxcomb.
Y. Ped. I rejoice in the irony. To be called coxcomb by a woman is as sure a sign of sense, as to be called a rogue by a courtier is of honesty.[64]

Fielding also reflected some of the confusion that was characteristic of the eighteenth century's use of *irony* and *raillery*. In *The Fathers, or The Good Natur'd Man,* a character uses the term *raillery* for what is obviously blame-by-praise irony. Sir George Boncour and his brother are discussing the outrageous conditions under which Mr. Valence will allow his daughter to marry Boncour's son:

Sir Geo. Aye, surely, no one can give another a stronger hint to impose upon him than by first imposing upon himself; you have infinite obligations to him, I think, for he sees you have an inclination to beggary, and therefore would make you a beggar. Besides, can anything be more reasonable than what he proposes? I am sure I should not expect such gentle terms in the same case! What doth he desire of you more than to throw yourself on the bounty of your son? Well, and who the devil would make any scruple of trusting a son, especially such a son as yours – a fine gentleman – one who keeps a wench – Never fear, man, I warrant he'll allow you pocketmoney enough.
Bonc. Raillery, Sir George, may exceed the bounds of good nature, as well as good breeding; I did not expect that you would have treated the serious concerns of my family in so ludicrous a manner, nor have laughed at me when I ask'd your advice.[65]

[63]   *Works* (Henley), X, p. 40.
[64]   *Works* (Henley), VIII, p. 108.
[65]   *Works* (Henley), XII, p. 186.

And in the "Essay on Conversation", Fielding himself employs both *raillery* and *banter* as blame-by-praise irony.

> True raillery indeed consists either in playing on peccadillos, which, however they may be censured by some, are not esteemed as really blemishes in a character in the company where they are made the subject of mirth; as too much freedom with the bottle, or too much indulgence with women, etc.
> Or, secondly, in pleasantly representing real good qualities in a false light of shame, and bantering them as ill ones. So generosity may be treated as prodigality; economy, as avarice, true courage as foolhardiness; and so of the rest.[66]

It should be noted, finally, that even in Fielding's attitude toward the effectiveness of irony is reflected some of the same concern of his contemporaries over the clarity of the ironist's intentions. Indeed, so conscious was he of the danger of irony backfiring on the ironist that in the *Jacobite's Journal* for March 26, 1748 he announced his intention of abandoning the ironic mask of an ardent Jacobite, John Trottplaid, Esq., that he had sustained for several months and, in the future, to attack the Jacobites directly.

> I have observed that, though irony is capable of furnishing the most exquisite ridicule, yet as there is no kind of humour so liable to be mistaken, it is of all others the most dangerous to the writer. An infinite number of readers have not the least taste or relish for it, I believe I may say do not understand it; and all are apt to be tired, when it is carried to any degree of length.[67]

But these fears were not present in Fielding's early works. Indeed, an examination of the techniques that he actually used in these works – whether or not he was always conscious of them as irony – suggests infinitely more boldness than caution.

---

[66] *Works* (Henley), XIV, p. 276.
[67] Quoted in F. Homes Dudden, *Henry Fielding, His Life, Works, and Times* (Oxford, 1952), I, pp. 558-9. Fielding did not, fortunately, adhere to this resolution, as *Tom Jones* so effectively illustrates.

II

RHETORICAL IRONY
I: THE IRONIC MASK

A. THE TECHNIQUE

In his early writings, Fielding employs two types of rhetorical poses that were fairly common to the 18th century: the non-ironic pseudonym, such as Addison and Steele used in the *Spectator*, and the ironic mask or *persona*, such as Swift used in *A Modest Proposal*. With the pseudonym, the reader is always aware that he is listening to Henry Fielding speaking directly to him, for the impersonation does not extend beyond the assumption of a false name. In the April 5th issue of *The Champion*,[1] for example, Captain Hercules Vinegar defends charity as a cardinal Christian virtue. But both the substance and the style of the essay testify to the fact that this is Fielding himself discussing seriously one of his favorite topics.

When he dons the ironic mask, he disguises himself not simply behind another name but behind a personality possessing easily identifiable characteristics. Ideally, however, the disguise is never perfect, for the reader must always be conscious of the difference between the two voices, Fielding's and the *persona's*. As with all irony, the deception must ultimately be seen.[2] Thus, when Field-

---

[1] Since all of the *Champion* essays relevant to this study were written by Fielding during the twelve-month period from November, 1739 to October, 1740, I shall list only the month and day when referring to specific issues.
[2] There is, however, one instance in *The Champion* where the mask is too convincing. On January 10, 1739-40, Fielding published a letter from "Philalethes" attacking The Champion, Captain Vinegar. The irony is so subtle here that if it were not for a note appended to the essay, the reader could easily take it at its face value. The presence of this note suggests

ing calls himself Job Vinegar and pretends to relate his curious experiences in the land of the Ptfghsiumgski, or the Inconstants, he creates a life-like character who is distinct from the author we know as Henry Fielding; Job Vinegar is an *almost* credible narrator. Yet the impersonation, unlike that of Gulliver, is never so convincing that we can ever completely separate Job from Fielding, whose presence we must always be able to sense behind the mask.

The *persona* usually embodies the specific vice, human foible, or stereotypic attitude that Fielding is attempting to expose and which is manifested in a number of different ways as the work develops. Indeed, one of the pleasures in listening to such a fictitious narrator stems from our awareness of the gradual unfolding of his personality. An important aspect of this process involves, as with Swift's *personae* in particular, some form of self-betrayal, which in turn helps undermine not only the fictitious narrator's doctrinal poses but his character as well. A dual satiric function is thus always present. Since Fielding's use of the ironic mask is usually confined to relatively short works (*The Voyages of Mr. Job Vinegar* and *Tom Thumb* are possible exceptions), this unfolding must be accomplished rapidly and with the kind of economy that Swift in *Gulliver's Travels*, for example, did not find necessary.

The presence of a *persona* also alters markedly the context of the irony, if not the rhetorical aim, of Fielding's satires, for he presents us not simply with a series of ironic statements that must be reversed or altered in some way in order for us to perceive his real meaning, but with a series of statements that defines the intellectual character of a fictitious author. It is this definition of a unique and clearly identifiable character that adds a new dimension to the often more readily apparent irony of the statements themselves, for their ultimate ironic value is now as much a result of the peculiar nature of the speaker as it is of the statements *per se.*

---

that Fielding (or possibly Ralph, his chief collaborator) recognized this danger too. The attack was really directed at Walpole.

B. THE PURPOSES OF THE MASKS

The ironic mask appears once in the plays – in *Tom Thumb* – not at all in the 1743 *Miscellanies, Shamela,* or *Joseph Andrews,* but on numerous occasions in *The Champion.* The narrators of *Joseph Andrews* and *Jonathan Wild* are not *personae* in the sense in which I have employed the term above. In each of these early novels, Fielding assumes an ironic pose but speaks always in his own voice. The personality of the narrator in each instance never emerges as distinct from Fielding's. (The self-conscious narrator in *Joseph Andrews* is discussed more fully in the conclusion.)

In *Tom Thumb,* the mask is both a continuation of the Popeian spoof on pedantry and captious criticism in the *Dunciad Variorum* and *Peribathous,* as well as a significant part of Fielding's own vitriolic and sustained struggle against "vice and imposture" in the theater. However, essential as it is to an understanding of *Tom Thumb,* the ironic mask is of relatively minor importance in the plays as a whole. It involves, after all, the kind of authorial intrusion that is inappropriate to 18th-century drama. Nevertheless, when considered together with the several important masks of *The Champion,* Scriblerus Secundus, the fictitious editor of *Tom Thumb,* is an important introduction to Fielding's use of this technique to satirize certain 18th-century stereotypes.

In *The Champion,* on the other hand, the ironic mask is of much greater significance in sustaining the satiric aim of Fielding's first newspaper. It is clearly one of his favorite techniques, for of the eighty-one essays Fielding wrote between November 1739 and October 1740,[3] thirty-four make extensive use of irony; and of

---

[3] As the basis for my study of *The Champion,* I have examined all of the essays signed with the letters "C" and "L" which are generally accepted to have been Fielding's signatures. I have not read the five signed essays published between July 15 and October 21, 1740. These have never been positively identified as Fielding's nor have they ever been reprinted. In addition, I agree with Professor Cross that Fielding was responsible for the unsigned essays on the following dates: November 15, 17, 20, and 22, February 28, May 6, 15, and 20, and June 17. Whatever Fielding wrote in addition to these (with the exception of *The Voyages of Job Vinegar*) is still a matter of conjecture.

these, twelve – over a third – employ *personae*,[4] not all of whom, it should be noted, are developed with equal care and consistency. Unlike *Tom Thumb,* most of the *Champion* essays were written quickly, seldom if ever revised before going to press, and, of necessity, relatively short – all factors which, ordinarily, would tend to militate against the use of the ironic mask. Despite these limitations, Fielding does depend on the ironic mask as an important vehicle for his satire, particularly in the essays of December 10, January 5, February 28, and in the related series of essays that appeared between March 20 and October 2 (*The Voyages of Mr. Job Vinegar*).

In these, as well as in the other essays that Fielding contributed to *The Champion* in 1739-40, his chief incentive was not disgust with political ineptitude and mismanagement as such, but with the old problems of "vice and imposture" in society as a whole. Unlike many of the Opposition critics, Fielding was more concerned with perversions of morality than with specific political issues, probably because he saw political corruption primarily as a manifestation of England's moral decline. Indeed, this was precisely the line that the Opposition papers – *The Craftsman* and *Common Sense* – had been taking in the late 1730's, a line which had, in turn, been echoed time and again by Opposition writers who were convinced – as James L. Clifford has pointed out – that "the old national vigor and simple honesty were fast disappearing. With no immediate hope for a change, the future of England was black indeed." [5] It is significant that in *The Champion* Fielding attacked Walpole more for the Prime Minister's alleged dishonesty than for his administrative policies. Most of the political

---

[4]   They are used on the following dates: November 15 (Captain Hercules Vinegar, The Champion himself), December 10 (The public defender), December 25 (the utilitarian educator), January 5 (the political extremist), January 12 (the political opportunist), January 26 (the pragmatist I), January 28 (the pragmatist II), February 28 (the political projector), May 15 (Belinda, the feminist in politics), May 20 (the drunkard defending drink), June 10 (the modern educator), March 20 and June 28 through October 2 inclusive (Job Vinegar, the obtuse world traveller).

[5]   James L. Clifford, *Young Samuel Johnson* (London, 1955), pp. 186-7.

hatchet-work was done by James Ralph, Fielding's chief assistant.[6]

The individual essays support this. Of the twenty-seven essays that deal directly or inferentially with, or merely have occasional references to, politics, not one deals exclusively with current political issues. Invariably, politics is simply the pretext for a discussion of broader moral issues. The remainder of the eighty-one essays are concerned with ethics, social foibles, and literary criticism (mostly attacks on Colley Cibber).

Generally implicit in these essays was a plea to men to eschew the values Walpole represented and to reestablish morality and integrity in government and, eventually, in society as a whole. In Captain Hercules Vinegar's justification of his court of judicature (December 22nd), Fielding underlines quite explicitly just such an aim.

How useful, and indeed how necessary this bench must be, will not be doubted by any who consider that our laws are not sufficient to restrain or correct half the enormities which spring up in this fruitful soil. The man who murders, robs, or ravishes, is indeed punished with death. But there are invaders and destroyers of our lives and fortunes, and of the persons and honour of our women, whom no laws in being can any way come at.

Nor would it be enough that those greater crimes should be punished, the covetous, the prodigal, the ambitious, the voluptuous, the bully, the vain, the hypocrite, the flatterer, the slanderer, call aloud

---

[6] John F. Speer, "A Critical Study of The Champion". Unpublished Ph.D. dissertation, Dept. of English, University of Chicago (1951), p. 232. When they did take up specific issues, Fielding and Ralph assumed the usual opposition stance vis-à-vis the Walpole ministry and took up the same charges that *The Craftsman* and *Common-Sense* had developed: Walpole's corrupt practices and their effects on England; his destruction of trade to humble the merchants; the government's avoidance of war because of Walpole's alleged subservience to Spain; and Walpole's fostering of Hanoverian interests in preference to England's (Speer, pp. 180-81). Of these, Fielding concerned himself only with corruption, allowing Ralph to discuss the others. The significance of Fielding's position rests on the fact that, with the exception of the corruption charge, the others were probably little more than opposition propaganda. (E.g., see John H. Plumb, *Sir Robert Walpole, The Making of a Statesman*, Boston, 1956, pp. 326-8.) On legitimate issues, such as the limitation of a standing army and triennial parliaments, Fielding made occasional comments, but his major political criticism dealt with dishonesty and corruption in government.

for the champion's vengeance. In short, whatever is wicked, hateful, absurd, or ridiculous, must be exposed and punished before this nation is brought to that height of purity and good manners to which I wish to see it exalted.[7]

The essays using ironic *personae* uphold this high moral purpose inasmuch as they constitute Fielding's bitterest attacks on those who most clearly contributed to England's moral decline. These essays also demonstrate the efficacy of the doctrine that the reinforcement of precept with example is the most effective means of implementing the didactic function of literature. To rouse people out of the moral complacency into which they had fallen, it was necessary, Fielding believed, not only to preach morality, but, more significantly, to show them morality and immorality in action.[8] Each of the *Champion personae* embodied some false value that Fielding deplored; each was a vivid personification of some form of affectation, immorality, or intellectual perversion.

Although the ironic masks in *The Champion* are, as I have indicated above, not all perfectly conceived, there are several which do merit close examination. Although Fielding attacks many people in *The Champion* – Walpole and Cibber most frequently – his best *personae* are the four who are employed on the dates mentioned above,[9] – the public defender, the political extremist, the projector, and, finally, the traveller – all, since recognition of the

---

[7] *Works* (Henley), XV, pp. 112-113.
[8] In the dedication to Lord Chesterfield of *Don Quixote in England*, Fielding asserts that "examples work stronger and quicker on the minds of men than precepts. – This will, I believe, my Lord, be found truer with regard to politics than to ethics: the most ridiculous exhibitions of luxury or avarice may likewise have little effect on the sensualist or the miser; but I fancy a lively representation of the calamities brought on a country by general corruption, might have a very sensible and useful effect on the spectators" (*Works*, [Henley], XI, p. 7).
Even the *Grub-Street Journal* (April 22, 1736) praised Fielding for his use of example rather than precept only in his attack on corrupt politicians in *Pasquin*: "The surest way to render all such persons ridiculous, and consequently despised, is to introduce them personated upon the stage, and there openly acting those vile parts, which they daily act in a more clandestine manner upon the stage of the world. This the author of *Pasquin* has done. . . ."
[9] See p. 34.

persona qua persona was so essential for the reader, defined in varying degrees by the social and literary conventions of the day. The remainder of this chapter will, therefore, focus on these fictitious authors – in addition to Scriblerus Secundus – since these five are the most dramatically effective of Fielding's early ironic masks.

C. THE MASKS

1. *The Editor*

The nature of the satire in the final (1731) version of *Tom Thumb* must certainly have governed in part Fielding's choice of the *persona* as a major ironic device in that play. *Tom Thumb* is an attack not only on the language and situations of heroic drama, but on undiscriminating, captious critics as well. The many allusions to Dryden, Bentley, and Dennis in particular in the prolegomena and notes, and the excessive ironic praise lavished upon them by Scriblerus Secundus, the play's "learned" editor, make quite apparent Fielding's purpose in employing an ironic mask in *Tom Thumb*. As an exaggerated embodiment of ineptitude, dullness, and pedantry, Scriblerus Secundus, a literary descendant of a more distinguished dunce, Martinus Scriblerus, is a composite of those faults that Fielding found most ridiculous in Restoration and 18th-century drama critics in general and John Dennis in particular.[10] The faults that had been attributed to Dennis, however, had also been attributed to many other critics of the late 17th and early 18th centuries.[11] Again and again critics were characterized as unprincipled people motivated by malice or envy. Good as well as bad critics were commonly lumped together as "dull, unimaginative, pedantic, impolite, lacking in candor and refinement, ill-natured, malicious, and envious".[12] As such, they were an even

[10]   James T. Hillhouse, ed., Introduction to *The Tragedies of Tragedies* by Henry Fielding (New Haven, 1918), pp. 37-9.
[11]   E. N. Hooker, ed., Introduction to *The Critical Works of John Dennis* (Baltimore, 1943), II, liv.
[12]   *Ibid.*

greater menace, it was believed, than bad poets. To Pope, for example, the very worst a bad poet can do is merely "tire our patience", whereas bad critics, he added, can "mislead our sense",[13] a cardinal sin to an age that valued above all else an intellect untrammeled by cant or obfuscation.

The prevalence of this attitude toward critics was probably as much the inspiration for the creation of the ironic mask, Scriblerus Secundus, as Fielding's enmity toward a particular few critics. The result is a composite picture of a critic who has no sense of literary propriety or decorum, delights in meaningless semantic quibbles, is inept in his use of the classical authors, and who bases his critical pronouncements on the most dubious criteria. Scriblerus Secundus is, in short, the very incarnation of the hypothetical bad critic Pope describes in the second part of the *Essay on Criticism*.[14]

The only barb that is aimed exclusively at Dennis is Fielding's ridicule of Scriblerus' chauvinism, a fault for which Dennis was particularly notorious.[15] Although there are allusions to it elsewhere in the play, it is perhaps most clearly reflected in the final note to the "tragedy", where Scriblerus insists that the presentation of battles on stage has inspired England's armies to victory over the French.

No scene, I believe, ever received greater honours than this. It was applauded by several encores, a word very unusual in tragedy. – And it was very difficult for the actors to escape without a second slaughter. This I take to be a lively assurance of that fierce spirit of liberty which remains among us, and which Mr. Dryden, in his essay on Dramatic Poetry, hath observed – 'Whether custom (says he) hath so insinuated itself into our countrymen, or nature hath so formed them to fierceness, I know not; but they will scarcely suffer combats, and other objects of horror, to be taken from them.' – And indeed I am for having them encouraged in this martial disposition: nor do I believe our victories over the French have been owing to anything more than those bloody spectacles daily exhibited in our tragedies, of which the French stage is so entirely clear.[16]

---

[13]   "Essay on Criticism", ll. 1-4.
[14]   Scriblerus also resembles, to a lesser degree, the pedants described briefly by Addison in *Tatler* 158 (April 13, 1710).
[15]   Hillhouse, p. 39.
[16]   *Works* (Henley), IX, p. 71.

The Scriblerian method of analysis is no less absurd. Like Pope's incompetent critic, and like the dunces of *Dunciad* IV, whose education consists primarily of learning words, Scriblerus equates critical judgment with verbal definition. To understand this "little piece", Scriblerus has "for ten years together read nothing else; in which time, I think, I may modestly presume, with the help of my English dictionary, to comprehend all the meanings of every word in it".[17]

He disqualifies himself as a critic in other obvious ways. He misses, for example, the point of Pope's stricture that the critic must either "Drink deep, or taste not the Pierian Spring".[18] He follows critical custom by relying heavily on the authority of the ancients, but his incompetence as a classical scholar underscores heavily the absurdity of his judgments. Fielding has him mistranslate, misinterpret, and even misquote, all with the flamboyant self-confidence of a Dennis or a Bentley. Thus, following one of the jokes of Pope's *Peribathous*, Fielding has Scriblerus mistranslate Ovid's "*Omne genus scripti gravitate tragedia vincit*" as "Tragedy hath, of all writings, the greatest share in the bathos." [19] And in a footnote to the text of *Tom Thumb*, Scriblerus justifies the employment of ghosts in tragedy by insisting that the Latin "fabula" means "ghost" as well as "fable" or "plot".

Of all the particulars in which the modern stage falls short of the ancient, there is none so much to be lamented as the great scarcity of ghosts. Whence this proceeds, I will not presume to determine. Some are of opinion, that the moderns are unequal to that sublime language which a ghost ought to speak. One says ludicrously, that ghosts are out of fashion; another, that they are properer for comedy; forgetting, I suppose, that Aristotle hath told us, that a ghost is the soul of tragedy; for so I render the ψυχὴ ὁ μῦθος τῆς τραγῳδίας which M. Dacier, amongst others, hath mistaken; I suppose misled by not understanding the Fabula of the Latins, which signifies a Ghost as well as a Fable.[20]

This is, however, not a simple mistranslation, for Scriblerus is not

17 *Ibid.*, IX, p. 8.
18 "Essay on Criticism", l. **216.**
19 *Works* (Henley), IX, **p. 12.**
20 *Ibid.*, IX, p. 55.

"simply" ignorant. He knows enough Latin to be able to confuse *fabula* with *manes* (which does mean "ghosts, departed spirits") from *fabulae manes*, a phrase used by Horace, among others, and in all likelihood, therefore, quite familiar to a cultivated Augustan reader.

Elsewhere, Scriblerus misinterprets (rather than mistranslates) a passage from the *Ars Poetica* (ll. 89-98) in order to lend authority to his preposterous assertion that "the greatest perfection of the language of a tragedy is, that it is not to be understood".[21] (This is part of the attack on bombast in heroic drama.) On the same occasion, he reveals a weakness that Fielding will later – in the *personae* of *The Champion* – elevate to a major intellectual flaw – a failure to perceive the figurative values of language. Here Scriblerus ignores (or, perhaps, fails to see) the common figurative meaning of *sermone pedestri* (plain speech, or the language of prose) and translates *pedestri* literally (one who must travel on foot – i.e., a person too poor to own a horse.) Thus, *sermone pedestri* is, literally rendered, the language of "the poorer sort of people only",[22] a gross perversion of Horace's original meaning. And on yet another occasion, he tampers with the original words of a quotation from Cicero's *De Oratore* in order to make Cicero seem to support Scriblerus' own predilection for "big-sounding words in tragedy".[23]

Equally exasperating to the reader is Scriblerus' insistence that precedents are sufficient justification for whatever may occur in this or any other modern play. This is, of course, part of the overall joke of *Tom Thumb*, for the most absurd lines and situations in the play are deliberate parodies of popular heroic dramas of the day.[24] Whatever the advantages of employing precedents, how-

---

[21] *Ibid.*, IX, p. 11.
[22] *Ibid.*, IX, p. 12.
[23] *Works* (Henley), IX, p. 12. The original was: *Quid est enim tam furiosum, quam verborum, vel optimorum atque ornatissimorum sonitus inanis, nulla subjecta sententia, nec scientia?* (*De Oratore*, I. xii. 50-1. This is the only Latin quotation which Mr. Hillhouse was unable to locate.) Fielding changes this to: *Quid est tam furiosum vel tragicum quam verborum sonitus inanis, nulla subjecta sententia neque scientia?*
[24] Fielding may have been imitating William Wagstaffe's use of the same

ever, their use by Fielding does help to establish an ironic tension within the play by focusing upon the contrast between the absurdity of the parallels and the seriousness with which Scriblerus employs them to justify the dramatic practices of the supposedly anonymous author of *Tom Thumb*. In the play's opening scene, for example, Noodle tells Doodle that

> They tell me it is whispered in the books
> Of all our sages, that this mighty hero,
> By Merlin's art begot, hath not a bone
> Within his skin, but is a lump of gristle.

To this speech Scriblerus appends the following note:

"To whisper in books," says Mr. D—s, "is arrant nonsense." I am afraid this learned man does not sufficiently understand the extensive meaning of the word Whisper. If he had rightly understood what is meant by the "senses whisp'ring the soul," in the Persian Princess, or what "whisp'ring like winds" is in Aurengzebe, or like thunder in another author, he would have understood this. Emmeline in Dryden sees a voice, but she was born blind, which is an excuse Panthea cannot plead in Cyrus, who hears a sight.
– Your description will surpass
All fiction, painting or dumb shew of horror,
That ever ears yet heard, or eyes beheld.
When Mr. D—s understands these, he will understand whispering in books.[25]

In a later note, Scriblerus uses a speech from one of Dennis' own plays as justification for a bad pun in *Tom Thumb*. When the king threatens to kill the ghost who visits the royal bedchamber (Act III, sc. ii), the latter counters with "I am a ghost and am already dead." Scriblerus notes Dennis' comment on the line:

"The man who writ this wretched pun," says Mr. D., "would have picked your pocket:" which he proceeds to shew not only bad in itself, but doubly so on so solemn an occasion. And yet in that excellent play of Liberty Asserted, we find something very much resembling a pun in the mouth of a mistress, who is parting with a lover she is fond of;

---

technique in the latter's earlier *Comment Upon the History of Tom Thumb* (London, 1711).
[25] *Works* (Henley), IX, pp. 19-20.

UL. Oh, mortal woe! one kiss and then farewell.
IRENE. The Gods have given to others to fare well.
    O miserably must Irene fare.[26]

This characterization of a foolishly pedantic editor, sustained consistently throughout the preface and the mock scholarly apparatus of the play itself, adds a significant dimension to the satire of *Tom Thumb*, for not only does Fielding hold up to ridicule the inanities of heroic tragedy, but he projects those inanities to us through the warped vision of an intellectually inept commentator, somewhat as Swift does in *Gulliver's Travels*, and more clearly as Pope does in the *Dunciad Variorum*, upon which the 1731 version of *Tom Thumb* was apparently modeled. As in his rehearsal plays, however, Fielding relies upon the relationship of the ironic frame to the action of the play to convey the chief ironic impact of the work, for, aside from Scriblerus' ludicrous blunders as a critic, his most serious defect is his failure to perceive the most obvious thing about the play proper – that it is a satire – a fact that would be immediately apparent to any ordinary reader acquainted with heroic tragedy, let alone someone pretending to have the critic's superior powers of observation and insight. What this immediately suggests is that Fielding's satiric quarry in *Tom Thumb* is more than just the bad play and the bad critic, but the reader and admirer of heroic tragedy who cannot distinguish the true thing from its parody. The mock tragedy and the mock editorial apparatus, then, become as much a comment upon this type of reader as it is upon the conventions of heroic tragedy itself, and a significant foreshadowing, to be sure, of Fielding's later attack on the readers of Richardson's *Pamela*.[27]

2. *The Public Defender*

One of the most curious of Fielding's early *personae* – and in some respects the most subtle – was that which he created for the

---

[26] *Ibid.*, IX, p. 56.
[27] In addition to *Shamela*, notice in particular the attitude of the ironic narrator of *Joseph Andrews* toward the sentimental reader who becomes so emotionally caught up in the story that he fails to see that at times he himself is an object of satire.

Champion of December 10th. In this essay, Fielding adopts the
mask of a smug, self-appointed defender of public morality and of
the theater Licensing Act which had been in effect now for some
eighteen months. Ordinarily, Fielding's *personae* are satiric characterizations of types or of particular people. In this essay, however, Fielding uses the mask to attack simultaneously those two
groups who were most responsible for the Licensing Act that drove
him out of the theater in 1737 – the London merchants, led at
this time by Sir John Barnard, and the Walpole administration.
Although the Licensing Act was already over a year old, Fielding
takes advantage here of the occasion of a new Covent-Garden
production by Theophilus Cibber of Buckingham's *The Rehearsal*
to attack anew the absurdity of censorship as well as the advocates
of the law.

The London merchants, reflecting the old Puritan quarrel with
the theater, were convinced that the theaters encouraged vice and
immorality and corrupted workers who would otherwise remain
honest and industrious. The merchants were particularly concerned when playhouses were established in the commercial districts
of London. In their protests they often associated the establish-
ment of theatres with the increase of brothels. As Sir John Hawkins observed in his *Life of Samuel Johnson,*

> The merchants of London, then a grave, sagacious body of men,
> found that it was a temptation to idleness and pleasure that their
> clerks could not resist; they regretted to see the corruptions of
> Covent-Garden extended, and the seats of industry hold forth allure-
> ments to vice and debauchery. The principal of these was Sir John
> Barnard, a wise and venerable man and a good citizen: he, as a
> magistrate, had for such time been watching for such information as
> would bring the actors of Goodman's Fields playhouse within reach
> of the vagrant laws: but none was laid before him that he could,
> with prudence, act upon.[28]

In support of a bill which he proposed in the House of Commons
in March, 1734-5, to limit the number of theatres, Barnard attacked them for "corrupting the youth, encouraging vice and de-

---

[28] Sir John Hawkins, *The Life of Samuel Johnson, L.L.D.* (London,
1787), p. 73.

bauchery, and being prejudicial to trade and industry".[29] Another theatre, he contended, would only aggravate an already dis-
graceful situation.

Walpole, on the other hand, appeared less concerned with the
possible threat to morality which the theatres represented than
with the threat to the government of possibly seditious plays. In
fact, the difference in motives of the two groups was made quite
evident when Walpole attempted to amend Barnard's bill in order
to give increased powers to the Lord Chamberlain for its enforce-
ment; the merchants, fearing the precedent that would be thus
established by giving extensive powers of censorship to an officer
of the Court, objected so strongly that the Prime Minister's clause
was defeated and Barnard insisted on withdrawing his bill from
further consideration at that time.[30] There were, then, sharp differences of opinion as to how the theatres were to be curbed – differences which led to a breach between Walpole and the merchants.
Indeed, the defeat of the Walpole amendment was a serious rebuff
to the ministry. According to P. J. Crean, it was Fielding's *Pasquin* and *The Historical Register* – plays which antagonized both
groups in Parliament – together with the furor aroused over the
Golden Rump episode, that enabled Walpole in 1737 to propose a
new (and stricter) version of Barnard's original bill. At this point,
the merchants and the government joined forces and the Licensing
Act was quickly passed in June, 1737.[31]

Fielding's *persona* in this *Champion* essay represents both of
these groups who were thus finally united in opposition to the
theatre. He is first the self-righteous bourgeois who has allied himself with those of "the graver sort" to whom the passage of the
Licensing Act represented the triumph of morality over immorality. He is the merchant who is contemptuous of poets and actors,
whom he lumps together with "other idle people". These were
the only ones who objected to the Licensing Act, he points out,

---

[29] P. J. Crean, "The Stage Licensing Act of 1737", *Modern Philology*,
XXXV (1938), p. 243.
[30] John Loftis, *The Politics of Drama in Augustan England* (Oxford,
1963), p. 139.
[31] Crean, pp. 248-252.

whereas those who wished for a reformation of the theatre and of English morals in general were "wise and thinking men". To Fielding's *persona*, the theatre is characterized by "licentiousness" and he condemns it as a "growing evil", for which "the legislative power hath provided so good a remedy . . .". His immediate concern, however, is the threat to morality posed by the introduction of certain "new pieces of wit" into Cibber's production of *The Rehearsal*. This gives the *persona* an opportunity to wag a cautionary finger at the government and remind it of its moral obligations to the English people to keep "the utmost vigilance and . . . take the most effectual care that no infringements be made in so invaluable a law".

With his actual criticism of Cibber's production, however, the speaker's role shifts from that of a self-appointed guardian of public morality, who is concerned lest the government grow lax in its moral responsibilities, to that of a defender of the government's political position. The possible immorality of Cibber's interpolations in Buckingham's farce suddenly becomes of less significance than the possibility that they might provide material for an attack on the administration. Through his mask, Fielding ironically expresses fear of what the opposition writers might do with a particular interpolation of Cibber's – references to an army of hobbyhorses and a sham battle scene – for, as he says with undisguised chauvinism, "There certainly never was any army less the subject of mirth, to a true Englishman, than the present . . .". (The question of a standing army was, of course, a hotly contested political issue – the government defending its necessity, the Opposition attacking it because of fears that Walpole would use the army as a means of maintaining power.[32]) Theatrical immorality, then, becomes important not for its own sake, but only as a pretentious and insincere introduction to what is apparently a more vital concern – the dangers of sedition.

This shift in focus from morality to politics assumes larger, more ominous, dimensions when Fielding's *persona* shows that his zeal in defending the ministry causes him not simply to *ignore*

[32] Basil Williams, *The Whig Supremacy, 1714-1760* (Oxford, 1952), p. 204.

morality, but, even worse, to *pervert* it. His concern over Cibber's comments that he will take his play to "the other house" (Drury Lane) whose master is known to give money for anything [33] is motivated by a fear that this remark may be construed as an attack on a "public" person (obviously Walpole). Slander, he then asserts, is serious only when applied to a person in the public eye, for "the slandering of a private Gentleman [is] of no great consequence". The self-righteous moralist has thus easily slipped into the role of the politician hiding behind a double standard. The *persona* has himself assumed a mask which, ironically, is itself two-faced.

Fielding's purpose in creating his ambiguous *persona* becomes most apparent when compared to other Opposition protests. In the first place, Fielding is clearly following closely in the footsteps of Dr. Johnson who, in the preceding May, had published an ironic defense of the Licensing Act, entitled *A Complete Vindication of the Licensers of the Stage, from the Malicious and Scandalous Aspersions of Mr. Brooke, Author of "Gustavus Vasa"*. Dr. Johnson too had assumed an ironic mask as his chief method of satire in order to ridicule more effectively the new authority of the Licenser "to do that without reason, which with reason he could do before".[34] Johnson's *persona*, however, bears little resemblance to Fielding's, for Johnson donned the mask of a pamphleteer employed by Walpole, whereas Fielding's is an independent citizen expressing a private view. Johnson's *Complete Vindication* is, however, a clear precedent for this kind of protest.

Fielding's *Pasquin*, on the other hand, offers a precedent for the two-pronged attack on both politics and morality that we find in this *Champion* essay, for in the first part of *Pasquin* Fielding attacks the politicians, while in the second ("The Life and Death of Common Sense"), he attacks those hypocrites (Firebrand, Law, and Physic) who are posing as moralists. And *Shamela*, published some sixteen months after this *Champion* essay, suggests a certain predilection for this same method of ambiguous satiric characteri-

---

[33] The manager of Drury Lane, Charles Fleetwood, was notorious for his inept financial management of the theatre.
[34] *The Works of Samuel Johnson* (Oxford, 1825), V, p. 336.

zation, for Parson Williams is, as Sheridan Baker has observed, at once both Established Churchman and Methodist.[35] Fielding's decision to employ a double mask in the December 10th *Champion*, then, seems hardly fortuitous.

Of more immediate topical significance to Fielding's ironic essay are the earlier objections to the Licensing Act of active members of the Opposition in parliament. In the House of Lords, Lord Chesterfield protested strenuously against the passage of the act on the grounds that existing laws were sufficient to prevent immorality on the stage. Of particular relevance to Fielding's *Champion* essay is Chesterfield's accusation that the government was hiding behind charges of immorality in order to pass a law which was really aimed at preventing criticism of the government. Chesterfield argued that the sensitivity of ministers to implied criticism should never be allowed to become the occasion for censorship. "A public thief", he pointed out, "is as apt to take the satire, as he is to take the money, which was never designed for him." [36] In the House of Commons, Pulteney followed precisely the same line of attack.[37]

In creating this ironic mask, then, Fielding was merely following the earlier lead of Johnson, Chesterfield and Pulteney in attacking the inconsistency and insincerity of the Walpole administration. But, unlike the other Opposition spokesmen, Fielding chose to attack the two groups responsible for the passage of the act by donning a mask that would reflect at once both the merchants' self-righteousness and the government's hypocrisy.

3. *Two Politicians*

In assuming the masks of two political figures, Fielding shifts his sights to different, but equally dangerous, forms of intellectual perversity. Through these masks, he exposes the mentality of the

---

[35] Sheridan W. Baker, Jr., Introduction to *An Apology for the Life of Mrs. Shamela Andrews* by Henry Fielding (Berkeley, 1953), p. xvii.
[36] Quoted from Wilbur Cross, *The History of Henry Fielding* (New Haven, 1918), I, p. 231.
[37] Cross, I, pp. 229-30.

political extremist on the one hand, and, on the other, the political schemer or projector – the latter a common butt of Augustan ridicule.

Fielding assumed the first of these masks (on January 5th) in response to a specific episode in the interminable paper war between *The Gazetteer* and the opposition journals over the usefulness of a standing army. As such, this *persona* is a particularly good illustration of the skill with which Fielding employs this technique in responding to an immediate topical stimulus, in contrast to the stereotypic and less immediate stimuli that prompted most of the other masks. Earlier, the editors of *The Gazetteer* had warned that if any of their readers persisted in opposing a standing army, they (the editors) would "be shortly compelled to resort to the pillory and cart's tail". Fielding assumes here the mask of an extremist who would seriously defend this type of "persuasion". Ignoring the political issue that motivated the *Gazetteer's* comment, Fielding leaps immediately to its dangerous implications by creating a monstrous and perverse embodiment of militant political extremism.[38]

To this "author", the only positive method of solving a dispute is what he calls the *argumentum baculinum* (lit., the argument of the staff), for the "truth" in any dispute resides only in that argument which is supported by the greater force – a *reductio ad absurdum*, in effect, of the assumption underlying the *Gazetteer* warning. The origins of the *argumentum baculinum*, he asserts, can be traced to that time when "wild men and wild beasts lived together". It is civilization which represents the degeneracy of man, and particularly his evolution toward a greater rational control of his primitive impulses. Thus, the lowest ranks of society are to be exalted because they reason least and fight most, brutes are better

---

[38]   It is possible that Fielding was continuing his ridicule here of Pulteney whom he first attacked in *The Grub-Street Opera* for his hot temper. When Will (Pulteney) agrees to fight with Robin (Walpole), the latter replies: "No, no, I am for no fighting; it is but a word and a blow with William; he would set the whole parish together by the ears, if he could; and it is very well known what difficulties I have been put to to keep peace in it" (*Works* [Henley], IX, p. 245).

than philosophers, and arenas are preferable to universities as "institutions" of learning.

[This method of argument] still subsists among the lower rank, such who have least degenerated from that state, with whom it is at present no more than a word and a blow. Nor hath it been ever so much laid aside among the politer sort, but that, when propositions have been flatly denied, by the assertion of a little negative monosyllable which gives great offense to military ears, it hath been always esteemed, among men of honour, as the only method proper to convince an obstinate antagonist.[39]

Underlying much of the *persona's* defense of the dignity of force is a coldly pragmatic insistence that the efficacy of any method should really be determined by its effects. One has only to consider, he points out, the success of certain princes in maintaining peace.

... It also serves very commodiously to settle certain difficult points, which sometimes arise between them and their own subjects; when any claims have been laid to liberty or property, or clamours raised against oppression and such ridiculous things, an application to the *argumentum baculinum* hath immediately quieted all doubts, and given perfect satisfaction in the most perplexing cases.[40]

And it is this same pragmatism that underlies his insistence that the rule of law is based on force rather than on reason. "Was you to withdraw this mighty argument, all the reason in the world would not be able to support it."

Eventually, however, the pragmatist gives way to the chauvinist – a pose to which Fielding keeps returning in creating his *personae*, possibly because, like Johnson later, he felt that protestations of patriotism too often concealed the scoundrel. The *persona* becomes the selfless patriot whose ultimate concern is the welfare of the people of England.

... The *argumentum baculinum* ... will always stick close to that party which is uppermost; and, being properly handled by them, will not fail soon to remove all rancour and uneasiness in the multitude, and bring them without murmuring to submit to whatever burthen their betters shall, in their great wisdom, think fit to lay upon them. I know it will be answered, that such heart-burnings and grumbling

[39]   *Works* (Henley), XV, p. 138.
[40]   *Ibid.*, p. 139.

are of no consequence, but are thoroughly laughed at and contemned by all great men. To which I reply, I am not writing in favour of the powers, but of the people of the universe, whom I should rather see well threshed, than gulled, or tricked, and cheated, and laughed out of their liberties.[41]

This is the final position toward which the *persona* has been directing his argument. England's only hope for achieving political unity lies not in the leadership of the "great men" (such as Walpole) who will ignore her "heartburnings and grumbling", but in the *argumentum baculinum* – which, if it could be considered an effective means of political persuasion, must also be recognized as the very nadir of political action.

Subtly undermining this vindication of the social and political necessity of force and the denigration of man's reason, is the carefully organized, rational form his argument assumes. Every assertion is supported by a proof – perverse though it may be – and he proceeds meticulously from the origins of force to its applications in history to its legality and to its pragmatic value. His defense concludes with an apology to his readers: my real motive in exploring this matter, he suggests, is my concern for *your* welfare; I, personally, have nothing to gain. (This implicit echoing of the last words of Swift's economic projector of *A Modest Proposal* simply helps confirm Fielding's obvious debt to Swift and that satirist's use of the ironic *persona*.) What Fielding presents us with, then, is a carefully organized rhetorical exercise employing the very methods it deplores. The militant anti-rationalist, in his zealous attempt to nail down his point with absolute finality, assumes the pose of the meticulous rationalist. However convincingly, therefore, the editors of *The Gazetteer* may argue their case for a standing army, the greater the unwitting risk of self-betrayal.

For the *Champion* of February 28th, Fielding adopts the pseudonym of Nicodemus Bungle and the personality of a projector with a panacea for England's political ills. In form, Bungle's *Art of Prime-Ministry* – written as a letter to *The Champion* – is a parody

[41]   *Ibid.*, pp. 140-141.

of the popular, if minor, 18th-century georgic that described particular skills or "arts", from politics to nursing babies.[42] In aim, Bungle's scheme is most immediately an attack on politicians and political projectors, while ultimately it serves as yet another opportunity of lashing out at Walpole's corruption.

Bungle's attempt to define England's true "interests" at the beginning of his letter is an extension *ad absurdum* of the doctrine of political expedience so popular among political "realists".

> The Interest of this Island, is, I believe, chiefly to preserve a good Understanding between the King and his People: To maintain a very small Army and a very strong Fleet; to keep up the strictest Alliance with the Maritime Powers without making too great Concessions to them on the Article of Trade; to ballance Power as equally as possible on the Continent, and to hold the Scales ourselves; to stop the Current of a certain Potentate's Encroachments in the *Mediterranean*; and those of another in the *West-Indies*; to encourage our Manufactures at Home, especially the Wollen, by taking Measures to prevent the Exportation of Wool (which as I am told may be accomplished) and by diminishing the Taxes, and with them the Price of Labour; to prevent the Growth of Luxury, and to take the Opportunity of every Hour's peace to lessen the Debts of the Nation.[43]

Clearly, according to Bungle, the most expedient way of dealing with divergent interests is to satisfy everybody on every controversial issue, political and domestic. In this respect, Bungle is the eternal politician, anxious to be all things to all men.

Fielding's own views on England's "interests" – as expressed several years later by his spokesman in *Amelia*, Dr. Harrison – confirm his satiric intentions in this *Champion* essay.

[42]   The following, noted at random from the two decades preceding the publication of *The Champion*, are illustrative of the tradition: *The Art of Parliamenteering* (1722). – Andre Deslands, *The Art of Being Easy at All Times, and in All Places* (1724). – William Halfpenny, *The Art of Sound Building* (1725). – Alexander Pope, *The Art of Sinking in Poetry* (1727). – James Bramston, *The Art of Politics, in Imitation of Horace's Art of Poetry* (1729). – Soame Jenyns, *The Art of Dancing, A Poem in Three Cantos* (1729). – *The Art of Nursing* (1733). – *The Art of Life, A Poem* (1737). – Jonathan Swift, *The Art of Wenching, A Poem* (1737).
[43]   *The Champion: Containing a Series of Papers Humourous, Moral, Political, and Critical*, 2 vols. (London, 1741), I, pp. 314-15; hereafter referred to as *The Champion* (1741).

But if, on the contrary, [a minister] will please to consider the true interest of his country, and that only in great and national points; if he will engage his country in neither alliances nor quarrels but where it is really interested; if he will raise no money but what is wanted, nor employ any civil or military officers but what are useful, and place in these employments men of the highest integrity, and of the greatest abilities; if he will employ some few of his hours to advance our trade, and some few more to regulate our domestic government; if he will do this, my lord, I will answer for it, he shall either have no opposition to baffle, or he shall baffle it by a fair appeal to his conduct. Such a minister may, in the language of the law, put himself on his country when he pleases, and he shall come off with honour and applause.[44]

Bungle's scheme is to substitute his own lectures on *The Elements of Prime-Ministry, Chiefly Natural* for what he claims are the "useless" languages and sciences of the present school curriculum. There are eleven such elements:

1. Several Kinds of Whispers . . .
2. A very particular broad Grin . . .
3. A Stare which surprises and confounds . . .
4. *Coup de Maitre*, or an humble Petition from the Wolf to the Shepherd, to be made his Deputy . . .
5. Promises of all Sorts and Sizes . . .
6. Slanders of the blackest Kind . . .
7.8.9. Squeezes by the Hand, Bows, and Invitations to Dinner, illustrated by proper Emblems, the last of them by a Fellow baiting a Mouse-Trap . . .
10. Bribery . . .
11. The Art of Lie-Looking [by which the minister becomes master of his countenance and conceals fear and shame in particular. He wears kick-proof breeches and an *antipudorific lotion* to prevent his complexion from changing color].[45]

Beneath the relatively simply surface irony with which these eleven elements are enumerated – the undisguised absurdity of the elements is, after all, at sharp variance with the carefully maintained

[44] *Amelia* (London, 1930), II, pp. 230-1.
[45] *The Champion* (1741), I, pp. 316-17.

air of credibility that characterizes the rest of Bungle's letter – lies a
more subtle attempt to present Walpole as the only reliable champion of England's true interests, for whenever the prime minister is
mentioned elsewhere in *The Champion*, one or more of the elements is always associated with him. In the December 13th issue,
for example, the author of the vision speaks of seeing

a huge over grown fellow, with a large rabble at his heels, who huzza'd
him all along as he went. He had a smile, or rather a sneer in his
countenance, and shook most people by the hand as he past. . . . He
was a great magician, and with a gentle squeeze by the hand, could
bring any person whatever to think, and speak, and do what he himself desired. . . .[46]

And on May 10th, the "man in the Moon" describes what he has
seen on earth:

Were the intimacies which I have beheld between the dregs of the
people and a certain great man to be disclosed; were the whispers,
the kisses, the hugs, the squeezes by the hand, the dear Toms, the
Jacks, dear Wills, and the dear Bobs, that I have seen pass to be
exposed, it might become a question, whether the most hated men in
public life, might not, in retirement, be the most contemptible.[47]

A more positive indication of Fielding's intentions to use this letter
to *The Champion* as an attack on Walpole is the note that Fielding
himself appended to Bungle's proposals:

I could not refuse inserting the above Letter as I am willing to
encourage Genius and Industry, but I would advise my Friend
Nicodemus to travel abroad with his Nostrums; for I apprehend they
will meet with little Encouragement here, where we neither have nor
can have a Prime Minister. . . . The Privy Council and the Parliament
are the Ministers of the Kings of England, . . . It is the present
Happiness of the People of England, that his Majesty acts with the
Concurrence of these Councils, and we have no Reason to Fear that
we shall be obliged (to use the Language of Shakespeare in *Julius
Caesar*) to walk under the Great Legs of any Subject whatsoever.[48]

Finally, it was Fielding's firmly maintained belief that of all the
ills to which the body politic is heir, the most damaging is corrupt

[46]   *Works* (Henley), XV, pp. 100-101.
[47]   *Ibid.*, p. 306.
[48]   *The Champion* (1741), I, p. 318.

leadership. In its original form, he thought, England's political system was perfect in design, characterized by a carefully arranged system of checks and balances. Any unnatural element, such as a corrupt minister exerting unwarranted power, would unbalance the delicate machinery of government. In the *Champion* of May 8th, he observes

> I have often thought our first politicians have framed their schemes of government from the idea of this engine; for what are the several officers and magistrates, from the King to the constable, but the several wheels of state, in a subordinate manner, making up one grand machine, which, like a piece of clock-work in right order, moves steadily and regularly by fixed and certain laws?
>
> Now, as in the mechanical machine, if any body intervenes, which hath no function assigned it by the maker, it must necessarily disorder the operation, and in proportion to the weight and power of this intervening body, will be the confusion and disorder occasioned by it; the same must happen in the political, whenever any person intrudes into a place, where, by the original constitution of the government, he ought not to be; for nothing can move by the laws assigned it at its creation, unless what preserves the same form it had when those laws were assigned.[49]

To Fielding, therefore, England's political future rested upon her ability to expel the cause of the disorder so that the body politic could regain that state of purity where everything "moves steadily and regularly by fixed and certain laws".

Keeping Walpole in mind, then, as we read Nicodemus Bungle's proposal, it is apparent that the ultimate irony lies not so much in the scheme itself as in its implied results. If every man were to practice Bungle's "Art of Prime-Ministry", he would not simply make his own fortune, as Bungle has suggested; he would become another Robert Walpole. Behind Bungle's explicit proposal, therefore, is the implicit, but more invidious, suggestion that what England really needs most to solve her political problems – to restore her to a state of political health – are more Robert Walpoles. And it is on this – the real proposal – that the ultimate subtlety of Fielding's ironic mask rests.

[49] *Works* (Henley), XV, p. 301.

4. *The Traveller*

The Voyages of Mr. Job Vinegar [50] illustrates the only extended use of the ironic *persona* in *The Champion*. To describe the life and customs of the Inconstants, the strange inhabitants of a distant land, Fielding dons the mask of an itinerant ancestor of *The Champion*, Mr. Job Vinegar. Unlike Fielding's other *personae*, however, Job's is a lusterless personality; he is dull and often inept. Most conspicuous is his inability to measure what he sees against some set of normative values. If Hercules Vinegar, the editor of *The Champion*, was – as he so loudly proclaims – willing to engage in Herculean tasks in attacking vice and imposture and in defending virtue and justice wherever it could be found, Job Vinegar here is the ironic antithesis of his biblical namesake, for the patience through faith of the Old Testament Job becomes in this instance a patience and an acceptance born of little more than an almost total passivity. It is this fault in particular that undercuts his role as objective narrator, as the dispassionate observer of manners and customs.

Since there is evidence to suggest that Fielding wrote most of *The Voyages* well in advance of publication and left them with Ralph, his chief associate, to insert at specified intervals, the absence of specific topical allusions is understandable. Instead, *The Voyages* relies rather heavily on ideas and themes that Fielding had used during his most active period with *The Champion*.[51] *The Voyages* concentrates on moral and social corruption, affectation and hypocrisy, the decay of the educational process, and the lack of integrity among professional men and politicians. Walpole and his followers are common objects of Fielding's ridicule. But Fielding's chief concern, here as before, is with the espousal of false

[50] I have used the Augustan Reprint Society's publication (No. 67) of *The Voyages of Mr. Job Vinegar* from *The Champion (1740)*, ed. S. J. Sackett (Los Angeles, 1958); hereafter referred to as *Voyages*. The Voyages appeared on the following dates in 1740: March 20, June 28, July 17, 22, 31, August 5, 9, 16, 19, 29, September 4, 13, and October 2. The July 31st paper, as Mr. Sackett has fairly conclusively demonstrated, is most certainly by someone other than Fielding.

[51] Speer, p. 73.

values, represented in this case by a collective "deity" – M[O]NEY.
What is new is the perspective Fielding adds to his old ideas by a
new vehicle – an extended fictional framework.

Through Job, his spokesman, Fielding pretends he is talking
about a strange country in a distant corner of the world, but unlike Lilliput or Brobdingnag, the land of the Inconstants is a thinly-
disguised England, while some of the specific inhabitants are easily
identifiable. Job's value as a satiric device depends on his failure
to see this parallel between England and the land of the Inconstants.

Unlike the other *personae*, Job does not attempt to defend anything. The irony of his characterization lies entirely in the objectivity of his manner, for he is a traveller whose purpose in writing
is to relate, not persuade. Yet his failure to demonstrate even a
modicum of common-sense has the ultimate effect of reducing
The Voyages to a parody of the popular travel-book tradition, for
Job is, in essence, a Lemuel Gulliver reduced to the extremity of
sight without comprehension. After all, Gulliver may be ingenuous
in Lilliput and mad in Houyhnhnmland, but he is far from stupid.
Anyone who would thus accept these voyages as a serious narrative is no less gullible than Job Vinegar. Fielding uses these
Voyages, then, to attack not only the social and intellectual evils of
England but the whole travel-book tradition and the gullibility of
its readers as well. And nowhere is this point more effectively illustrated than in Captain Hercules Vinegar's introduction to Job's
narrative, for the introduction to the March 20th *Champion* is an
ironic defense of the fantastic voyage against the criticism of
skeptics.

No. 55, 20 March 1739/40

– *Mores Hominum multorum vidit.* – HOR.

There are a Sort of Men so sceptical in their Opinions, that they are
unwilling to believe any Thing which they do not see. I know a
Gentleman of good Sense in the Country, who hath never been farther
than at the Assizes which are held in his own County, who does not
believe that there are any such Diversions as Masquerades or *Italian*
Operas; he gives very little Faith likewise to the Accounts of Entertainments at the Play-Houses, the Custom of Visiting, and several
others; nay, upon my once telling him it was usual for lustly young

Fellows to give two Men a Shilling for carrying them in a Thing call'd a Chair from one Street to the other, he shook his Head with a disdainful Sneer, and cry'd, *Ay, persuade me to that if you can.*

This Infidelity hath been much complained of by Travelers, who, if they advance any Thing foreign to the Habits and Customs of our own Country, have often the Lie secretly given them by their home-bred Hearers, which want of Faith is so general that it hath given Rise to a Proverb; and when a Man would give you gently to understand that your Story meets with no Credit from the Company, it is usual to desire you *not to put the Traveller upon them.*

Those who have obliged the World with written Accounts of their Voyages, have very severely experienced this Temper, more especially those who have treated of remoter Countries, and such as few People know any Thing of besides themselves. Several excellent Accounts of *Asia* and *Africa* have been look'd on as little better than fabulous Romances. But if a Traveller hath the good Fortune to satisfy his Curiosity by the Discovery of any new Countries, any Islands never before known, his Reader allows him no more Credit than is given to the Adventures of *Cassandra,* or the celebrated Countess *Danois's Fairy Tales.* To omit Robinson Cruso, and other grave Writers, the facetious Capt. *Gulliver* is more admired, I believe, for his Wit than his Truth; and I have been informed, that several ignorant People doubt at this Day whether there be really any such Places as *Lilliput, Laputa,* &c.

Notwithstanding this Discouragement, I shall venture to give the Reader some Extracts from the Voyages of one of my Ancestors, and if I find they are well received by the Publick, may very probably some time or other present them with the whole Collection. I shall communicate them in the Words of my Ancestor.[52]

The comments of the ship's crew that accompanies Job support the satiric aim implied in this introductory paper by offering a subtle counterpoint to Job's obtuseness. Whenever they appear, the sailors always see beneath the surface of a situation, but are "corrected" by Job who sees *only* the surface, and who, like Swift's modern author in *A Tale of a Tub*, confuses the metaphoric with the literal. Representing worldly common-sense, the sailors are employed by Fielding to emphasize Job's lack of judgment. In the March 20th *Champion*, the crew sees the "pompous Diversions" for what they really are – perversions of religion and law respectively – but Job, who patronizingly excuses the sailors because they

"did not understand [the Inconstants'] language", judges these aspects of Inconstant culture by their appearance only. What are
clearly church services are to Job only theatrical performances:

> For the Representation of those Shews which our Crew fancied to
> have something of religious Worship in them, there are in every Town
> one or more large Edifices or Theatres, which are maintained at the
> publick Expence: In the largest of these, they generally perform their
> Operas; for which, besides a large Number of Voices, they maintain
> likewise several grave Persons at a more considerable Stipend, only
> to beat Time. Their other theatrical Representations are confined to
> so few Characters, that they are rather like Lectures than Comedies.
> And I have been told by several of the Natives, that some of them
> contain very excellent Lessons of Morality. The Magistrates go to
> them in Form, where, as it is often the only Vacancies they have
> from their above mentioned Councils, they all go to sleep; which,
> together with the Behaviour of most of the other Spectators, assures
> me there is nothing religious in their Meetings; for, indeed, the Be-
> haviour of the Performers would otherwise have inclined me to the
> contrary Opinion;

and legal proceedings are only public games:

> As to that Part of their publick Diversions, which our Men mistook
> for Law, it is a Game unlike any Thing practiced in *Europe*, and
> may be played by one or two, or sometimes ten of a Side. There are
> two Balls, one of which they call PLT, and the other DFT. The
> Gamesters are furnish'd with Rackets called BRFS, with which they
> beat the two Balls from one to the other; young robust Gamesters
> sometimes strike them away immediately, but those who are more
> experienced will keep them up till they are beaten to Pieces. As this
> is the most consummate Perfection in the Game, so they are reckoned
> the most dextrous Gamesters, who strike the Ball in such a Manner
> to the Adversary as he may be capable of returning it. There is some-
> times one and sometimes four Umpires of this Game; and if well
> played, it affords excellent Sport to the Spectators.[53]

In sharp contrast to Job, the sailors represent the norm of clear
vision which unobtrusively threads its way through the narrative.
That they are continually rejected by Job serves only to intensify
our impression of his blindness and of the irony of his position as
a whole.

[53]   *Ibid.*, pp. 2-3.

Job's literalism is a striking manifestation of his confusion of appearance with reality – a fault which, as Fielding continually emphasizes, Job shares with the Inconstants. In the March 20th issue, for example, where Job describes the methods of electing magistrates, the irony is as much the result of Job's perfectly sustained historical objectivity (an objectivity which, paradoxically in this instance, betrays the historian) as it is of the Inconstants' reversal of literal and metaphoric "weight".

These wise People have two Methods of electing their Magistrates, which are by Weight and Measure; for which Purpose, every Town hath a large Chair erected, and near it a Pair of Scales. No Man can be admitted to the Magistracy, till he is of such an exact Weight, and likewise fills the Chair: For which Reason, they have two Phrases to express their highest Opinion of their Countrymen, *viz. He fills his Post with great Ability.* Or, *He is a Man of great Weight in his Country.* By this Method they preserve an exact Symmetry among their Magistrates, who are call'd a CRPUS, or one Body, which Rule being likewise observed in their Dress, by them called ICK-PDDNG, strikes a very great Awe into the Eyes of the Beholders of their Processions.[54]

Indeed, so complete is Job's devotion to an objective representation of everything that he encounters in the land of the Inconstants that there are occasions when even the Inconstants appear to be amusing themselves at Job's expense. Notice, for example, his description of the Inconstants' learning, in the *Champion* for August 16th:

The greatest Curiosity which I saw there, was the 30000000000th Part of a Louse, which, tho' it was so very small that I could not distinguish it by the naked Eye, one of their learned Men cut it in two, and gave me one Half, telling me, that little Bit of Matter would find me Employment all my Life-time: but, by the Extremity of ill Luck, I dropt it out of my Pocket somewhere in St. *James's* Park, and tho', since my Return Home, I searched after it many Days, could never find it.[55]

Despite the absurdity of Inconstant learning, it would be difficult to deny the even greater folly of the narrator.

[54] *Ibid.,* p. 2; the italics are Fielding's.
[55] *Ibid.,* p. 22.

The August 5th *Champion*, in which Job accepts quite literally all feminine protestations of chastity, illustrates much the same thing. It is the clearsightedness of the crew in this instance which serves again to indicate the absurdly obvious and to emphasize Job's obtuseness.

As soon as this Month [the HNEY MON] is expired, it was the Opinion of our Crew, that the Wives became in common, but their Sages assured me of the contrary, and that a Man might go to Law for his Wife as well as for a Joint-Stool, or any other Utensil; and that a Man whose Wife was inconstant, was infamous among them. Indeed I observed in the Company of most married Women, that their Chastity was a favourite Topic of their Conversation, and that they expressed great Abhorrence of all their Sex who did not preserve what we call a virtuous Character, and a certain married Lady of no great Youth or Beauty, was so exasperated at my Addresses to her, that, whenever I sat at Table with her, she always trod on my Toes.[56]

At its farthest extreme, Job's blindness, like Gulliver's in Houyhnhnmland, takes the form of a total acceptance of Inconstant values. The Inconstants live in a world of inverted moral and intellectual values, where good is bad, ignorance is excellence, and hypocrisy is honesty. Very often Job makes generalizations based on just such perversions. In his description of their laws, for example (July 22), he adopts a typical Inconstant inversion of great and little:

All great Vices, as Drinking, Gaming, injuring their Neighbour by walking over his Land, or taking away a Cock or a Hen from him, etc. are very severely punished, but for little Foibles, and which may rather be called Weaknesses than Crimes, such as Avarice, Ingratitude, Cruelty, Envy, Malice, Falshood, and the rest of this Kind, they are entirely overlooked.[57]

And on another occasion (August 5th), he assumes a contemptuous attitude toward those who marry for love:

... Very ugly Women have often their Choice of the greatest and noblest Matches, while perfect Beauty is utterly disregarded, I mean amongst their religious People, for such profligate Wretches as *have*

[56]   *Ibid.*, p. 17.
[57]   *Ibid.*, p. 11.

no MNEY, marry here merely out of carnal Affections, and because they like one another, as they do in other Countries.[58]

And as with Gulliver at the Academy of Lagado, Job too gets so carried away with admiration for the Inconstant scientific experiments (August 16), that what began as unwitting acceptance of perverse values becomes here an active advocacy of those "Discoveries of a nice and useful Nature" – discoveries which, he suggests, might prove of great commercial benefit to England.

These few Experiments shall suffice, as they may well give the Reader an Idea of the whole Collection which is extremely voluminous, and, if translated into our Language, would be of great Advantage to Trade: As for Instance, to the Tallow Chandlers, who might learn to make Candles which would last the whole modern, Winter Evening *viz*, from four in the Afternoon, 'till four in the Morning, by observing the excellent Solution of the following Problem, *viz*. If you draw four Lines from A B C D at the Top, to E F G H at the Bottom, all of equal Length, so that these four Lines may form a Square; then make a Section, by a Line drawn exactly in the Middle at K, and that Part of the Square which is below the Line K, will be exactly equal to that which is above it. It follows, that if a Candle of 14 Inches will burn 6 Hours, one of 28 of the same Latitude will burn 12.[59]

Job here comes very close to the madness of his hosts, if, indeed, he does not surpass them.

Job's tendency to accept enticing surfaces, to trust to sense perceptions without ever feeling compelled to test those impressions against either experience or common sense, reflects, inversely, Fielding's concern – expressed elsewhere in *The Champion* – with man's persistent failure to distinguish appearance from reality. In *The Champion* for November 22nd, he is appalled at the complacent acceptance of the superficiality that he sees all about him. (There is no mask here, simply Fielding speaking out directly.) "It is a truly political Rule", he says, "to have regard to Appearances: Men are too lazy, and too timorous to search to the Bottom; and every Man may be thought to be, what he will only take the Pains to appear to be." [60] This concern with appearances, Fielding feels,

---

[58]   *Ibid.*, p. 15.

[59]   *Ibid.*, p. 22.

[60]   *The Champion* (1741), I, p. 21.

ultimately becomes a form of "blind Idolatry" which makes man more willing "to suffer Martyrdom, rather than forego an Error, that Fashion and Opinion have so long render'd venerable".[61] With Job, this "blind Idolatry" becomes elevated into a kind of *modus vivendi* – as indeed it does with most of Fielding's *personae*. And as Job never probes beneath the surface of the society that confronts him, so he cannot see how that surface invariably belies its interior.

If, however, "Men are too lazy, and too timorous to search to the Bottom" of things, then Job becomes more representative than unique, and his shallowness of vision becomes a national rather than a purely personal fault. What Fielding is demanding of his contemporaries, in effect, is that they see the consequences of their intellectual lassitude by showing them how English society (thinly veiled behind the allegory of the *Voyages*) appears when viewed not objectively but with an almost total passivity. Job becomes ultimately, then, a mirror image of the passive, docile Englishman who seldom, if ever, applies his common sense to an evaluation of his own society, but merely accepts and reflects and finally conforms. Such passivity becomes as dangerous to society, Fielding feels, as any form of social, moral, or political corruption, perhaps even more. Fielding's opening attack on skepticism, therefore (see pp. 56-57 above), is as ironic as his defense of the fantastic voyage, for skepticism is the very quality that is most needed to overcome the Englishman's "blind Idolatry" of appearances.

D. FIELDING AND SWIFT

The foregoing should make apparent that, at their best, Fielding's early ironic masks achieve a fairly high level of technical sophistication. And their success is attributable not simply to their function as satiric vehicles but to their effectiveness in lending added dimension to the works in which they appear. Fielding's success is limited, however, when we compare his *personae* to those incontestably brilliant characterizations of Swift's: the *personae* of *A Tale of a*

[61] *Ibid.*, p. 19.

Tub, A Modest Proposal, the *Argument Against Abolishing Christianity,* the *Drapier's Letters,* and *Gulliver's Travels.* And Swift's use of the *persona* must certainly be considered the ideal against which the practice of all other satirists must be measured.

For one thing, the characters of Fielding's early *personae* are never as concretely realized as Swift's. They are intellectual entities, quite distinct from Fielding, to be sure, and possessing readily identifiable characteristics of manner and thought, but we never get to know them very well as human beings, and this detracts from their ultimate effectiveness as satiric devices. Nowhere is this more effectively illustrated than in the contrast between the concluding arguments of Fielding's advocate of force in politics (*The Champion,* January 5th), and Swift's advocate of cannibalism as a means of economic expediency.

Fielding: I should not have recommended this way of arguing so strenuously, had not I seen the excellence of it in my own family; in which, very violent disputes were wont formerly to arise, tending only, as I observed, to create animosities between the parties, who, on these occasions, always departed more confirmed in their own opinions; on which account, I introduced this argument, [*i.e.,* the *argumentum baculinum*] and have been obliged to apply it with great force on both sides the question: but, at present, my whole family are so perfectly well acquainted with its weight, that, the warmest dispute, on whatever subject, or however far advanced, on my bare pointing to the argument, which I have formerly informed my reader hangs over my chimney-piece, ceases in an instant, every thing subsiding and being hushed, as the tempest in the first *AENEID* at the voice of Neptune.[62]

Swift: I profess in the Sincerity of my Heart, that I have not the least Personal Interest in endeavouring to promote this necessary Work, having no other Motive than the *Public Good of my Country, by advancing our Trade, providing for Infants, relieving the Poor, and giving some Pleasure to the Rich.* I have no Children, by which I can propose to get a single Penny; the youngest being nine Years Old, and my Wife past Child-bearing.[63]

The passage from *The Champion* most certainly has considerable charm, wit, and humor, but despite the allusions to his family and

---

[62]   *Works* (Henley), XV, p. 141.
[63]   Swift, *Works* (Davis), XII, p. 118.

their quarrels, Fielding gives us not a single concrete detail about the speaker's life beyond his ideas. The family remains an abstraction and only the staff – the central symbol of the speaker's argument in defense of force as the only effective means of political action – is given concrete existence: it hangs ominously over his chimney-piece as a constant deterrent to family bickering. *A Modest Proposal*, on the other hand, ends on a series of specific details that force us to focus on the economic projector as a concretely realized human being. It is through the simplest of concrete details – the single penny, the nine year old child, the middle-aged wife – that Swift climaxes with brilliant point not only the characterization of his *persona* but the complex irony of the proposal as a whole.

Fielding's masks fall short of Swift's in another way. The presence of the *persona* in a Fielding work is never so pervasive as to affect the very style of Fielding's prose. If the intellectual and personal nature of the speaker differs from work to work, the style is fairly consistent. If the *persona* does not speak with Fielding's voice, he does with his manner. This is not so with Swift, whose *personae*, as William B. Ewald has suggested, create their own styles, and in so doing, modify even Swift's style.[64]

Purely as a technique, the ironic mask undoubtedly attracted Fielding because of its affinity to the drama, and in these early works, he was still more the conscious dramatist than the periodical essayist or novelist. But in all of his *personae* there is clearly apparent that firm, conscious control of technique and that exuberance of mood and manner – more, admittedly, in some than in others – that characterize Fielding at his best. That they fall short of Swift's *personae* is, after all, more a tribute to Swift's mastery than an accurate gauge of Fielding's – or any other satirist's – inadequacies.

[64]   Ewald, p. 184.

RHETORICAL IRONY
II: THE TECHNIQUES OF VERBAL IRONY

There are seven basic techniques of verbal irony that appear with some frequency between Fielding's "Masquerade" (1728) and the 1743 *Miscellanies*. However, as should become apparent from the descriptions that follow, not all of these techniques are mutually exclusive. At times, it is difficult to draw absolute distinctions between certain of them – such as reversal of statement and irony by implication – for in practice they frequently cross one another, both in nature and function. And with others – such as denotative irony and reversal of statement – the distinction is primarily quantitative rather than qualitative. But for purely descriptive purposes, it is possible to isolate these seven devices through which virtually all of the verbal irony in Fielding's early works is conveyed.

It should also be apparent that Fielding was strongly dependent upon the practices of contemporary ironists. Indeed, there is not one of these seven that is peculiar to his works alone. As one might expect, many of these techniques can be found in the satires of Swift in particular, who often employed them with an even greater sophistication than did Fielding; and other good 18th-century ironists – such as Pope and Defoe – employed certain of these devices with at least comparable success. Whatever originality Fielding can claim as an ironist rests upon his variations of several of the basic verbal forms, such as denotative and connotative irony.

With all of these forms of verbal irony, the context is the controlling factor which should insure the perceptive reader's correct response. Fielding, however, has provided us with a more explicit guide to certain of his verbal shifts in the series of ironic definitions in his "A Modern Glossary", published in the *Covent-Garden Journal* for January 14, 1752, a glossing of "such Terms as are at present greatly in Use" in the *beau monde*. "Fine", for example, is defined as:

An Adjective of a very peculiar Kind, destroying, or, at least, lessening the Force of the Substantive to which it is joined: As *Fine* Gentleman, *fine* Lady, *fine* House, *fine* Cloaths, *fine* Taste; – in all which *fine* is to be understood in a Sense somewhat synonymous with useless.

And "Great" is defined as a word which when "applied to a Thing, signifies Bigness; when to a Man, often Littleness, or Meanness".[1] Where applicable, definitions such as these provide a highly suggestive context for some of his earlier verbal ironies.

A. DENOTATIVE IRONY

In its simplest forms, Denotative Irony [2] corresponds to the rather common 18th-century technique implicit in the contextual uses of the word *irony* as direct praise [3] as well as to two popular techniques, blame-by-praise and praise-by-blame, that modern critics have associated with the works of other 18th-century ironists.[4] With denotative irony, Fielding uses a word whose denotation is either antithetical to or distinctly different from what he really means. It appears as blame-by-praise, praise-by-blame, and as a verbal inversion involving neither praise nor blame. In each case, all the reader is required to do is reverse or alter in some way the literal meaning of the word. When Fielding intends blame-by-praise, he selects a word whose denotation is either antithetical to his real meaning ("good" is really "bad") or different ("polite" is really "lazy"). But when he intends praise-by-blame, Fielding uses words with antithetical denotations only ("bad" is really "good"). With

---

[1] *Covent-Garden Journal*, I, pp. 154-6. The italics are Fielding's.
[2] I am indebted to Eleanor N. Hutchens' valuable essay, "Verbal Irony in *Tom Jones*", *PMLA*, LXXVII (Mar., 1962), pp. 46-50 for the terms "denotative" and "connotative" irony. In Fielding's early works, however, these techniques assume rather different forms than in *Tom Jones*.
[3] Knox, pp. 104-111.
[4] See chapter I, p. 23.

verbal inversion, however, the shift is again to either an antithetical denotation ("old" is really "young") or a different denotation ("shield" is really "saucer").

Fielding employs antithetical denotation (as blame-by-praise) to ridicule his own use of a burlesque simile in *Tom Thumb*. At the end of Act II, Huncamunca compares herself to

> ... some wild unsettled fool,
> Who had her choice of this and that joint-stool;
> To give the preference to either loth,
> And fondly coveting to sit on both:
> While the two stools her sitting-part confound,
> Between 'em both fall squat upon the ground.[5]

To this, Fielding (as Scriblerus Secundus) appends the following note to justify this coarse comparison:

This beautiful simile is founded on a proverb which does honour to the English language:
Between two stools the breech falls to the ground.[6]

The shift to denotations which are different from the real meaning adds a degree of subtlety to Fielding's use of denotative irony as blame-by-praise. Here the reader is forced to rely much more upon the context than before in order to perceive the irony, for the real meaning is drawn from a wider range of possibilities than is required for the shift to an antithetical denotation. In *Joseph Andrews*, Fielding employs the different denotation to puncture the pomposity of the doctor who condescends to explain the nature of Joseph's injuries to Parson Adams with the following gibberish:

"Sir," says the doctor, "his case is that of a dead man – The contusion on his head has perforated the internal membrane of the occiput, and divellicated that radical small minute invisible nerve which coheres to the pericranium; and this was attended with a fever at first symptomatic, then pneumatic; and he is at length grown relirius, or delirius, as the vulgar express it." [7]

Subsequently, Fielding describes this as the doctor's "*learned* manner". Now, this is not an *ignorant* or *unlearned* manner, but a

---

[5] *Works* (Henley), IX, p. 54.
[6] *Ibid.*
[7] P. 49 (I, xiv).

pseudo-learned manner which, in its perversion of legitimate medical terminology, becomes an abuse rather than an absence of learning, a denotative shift which is consistent with Fielding's later ironic definition of "learning" as "pedantry" in the "Modern Glossary".[8]

Praise-by-blame is a minor variation of denotative irony. In *The Champion* for November 17th, Captain Hercules Vinegar attacks "hereditary honour" and defends individual worth as the only criterion by which a man should be judged.

Hereditary Honour, considered abstractly, without any Regard to the Designs for which it was instituted, will appear as ridiculous as any Opinion which Time and Authority have given a Sanction to.[9]

Then, in an ironic vein, Captain Vinegar applies *scrub*, which Johnson defined as "A mean fellow", or as "Anything mean or despicable", to the merchant class who, though of humble descent for the most part, constitute what he considers to be the real source of England's strength as a nation.

I have often wondered how such Words as *Upstart, First of his Family*, etc. crept into a Nation, whose Strength and Support is Trade, and whose personal Wealth (excepting a very few immense Fortunes) is almost entirely in the Hands of a Set of sturdy SCRUBS, whose chief Honour is to be descended from *Adam* and *Eve*.[10]

Verbal inversion is easily distinguished from the preceding techniques if we bear in mind that it serves no evaluative function; it is used for neither blame nor praise. It is strictly a stylistic mannerism that helps establish the comic tonal quality of the particular passage in which it appears. In his description of Adams' rickety horse in Book II of *Joseph Andrews*, for example, Fielding ironically attributes to the horse a weakness of character ("foible") when in reality the horse suffers from no more than a predilection for kneeling, or weak knees, or even – if we cannot trust the literal meaning of "kneeling" – a tendency to fall or collapse. The denotative shift is thus to a different meaning.

---

[8]   *Covent-Garden Journal*, I, p. 156.
[9]   *The Champion* (1741), I, pp. 7-8.
[10] *Ibid.*, p. 10.

As soon as the passengers had alighted from the coach, Mr. Adams, as was his custom, made directly to the kitchen, where he found Joseph sitting by the fire, and the hostess anointing his leg; for the horse, which Mr. Adams had borrowed of his clerk, had so violent a propensity to kneeling, that one would have thought it had been his trade, as well as his master's: nor would he always give any notice of such his intention; he was often found on his knees, when the rider least expected it. This foible, however, was of no great inconvenience to the parson, who was accustomed to it; and as his legs almost touched the ground when he bestrode the beast, had but a little way to fall, and threw himself forward on such occasions with so much dexterity, that he never received any mischief; the horse and he frequently rolling many paces' distance, and afterwards both getting up, and meeting as good friends as ever.[11]

Fielding's description of Adams' arraignment before the justice in Book II illustrates the straightforward inversion to an antithetical denotation:

The clerk now acquainted the justice, that among other suspicious things, as a penknife, &c., found in Adams' pocket, they had discovered a book written, as he apprehended, in ciphers; for no one could read a word in it. "As", says the justice, "the fellow may be more than a common robber, he may be in a plot against the government – Produce the book." Upon which the poor manuscript of Aeschylus, which Adams had transcribed with his own hand, was brought forth. . . .[12]

"Suspicious", as it modifies the contents of Adams' pocket, is really "unsuspicious", with neither blame nor praise implied. This type of verbal inversion, however, acquires a degree of subtlety from the reflexive nature of the ironic modifier, which frequently directs implied blame or praise toward a quite different object in the same sentence or paragraph. Thus "suspicious" also reflects blame – and ultimately ridicule – back upon the fatuous clerk and justice of the peace who are attempting to transform Adams into a criminal.

What further complicates the verbal inversion is Fielding's practice of using both antithetical and different denotations as inversions of the same word. Perhaps nothing in his early works illustrates this as effectively as Fielding's ironic use of "favour" in

[11] Pp. 105-6 (II, v).
[12] P. 137 (II, xi).

Joseph Andrews. On one occasion – the visit of Adams, Joseph, and Fanny to the squire in Book III – it really means both "disfavour" (the antithetical denotation) as well as "trick" or "joke" (the different denotation).

> They arrived at the squire's house just as his dinner was ready. A little dispute arose on the account of Fanny, whom the squire, who was a bachelor, was desirous to place at his own table; but she would not consent, nor would Mr. Adams permit her to be parted from Joseph; so that she was at length with him consigned over to the kitchen, where the servants were ordered to make him drunk; a *favour* which was likewise intended for Adams; which design being executed, the squire thought he should easily accomplish what he had, when he first saw her, intended to perpetrate with Fanny.[13]

On another occasion – his description of the memorable night battle between Adams and Slipslop in the latter's bed – Fielding employs the word in a completely different sense. Here, "favour" ("service") really means both "disfavour-disservice" (the antithetical denotation) as well as "cuff" or "blow" (the different denotation).

> ... [Adams] therefore rescued the beau [Didapper], who presently made his escape, and then, turning towards Slipslop, received such a cuff on his chops, that his wrath kindling instantly, he offered to return the *favour* so stoutly, that had poor Slipslop received the fist, which in the dark passed by her, and fell on the pillow, she would most probably have given up the ghost.[14]

On occasion, Fielding varies his use of denotative irony by employing not a single word but the terminology associated with a body of knowledge or a particular activity, such as law, warfare, trade, or politics.[15] It is a technique that bears some resemblance to "allusive irony", the subtle blend of manners and attitudes that Reuben Brower has found characteristic of the satiric modes of Dryden and Pope.[16] It is also the verbal analogue to a mannerism that A. R. Humphreys has suggested is characteristic of much of Fielding's irony, a deliberate formalizing – after the fact – of an

---

[13] Pp. 236-7 (III, vii). Unless otherwise noted, the italics are mine.
[14] Pp. 332-3 (IV, xiv).
[15] Cf. referential irony in Hutchens, "Verbal Irony", p. 49.
[16] Brower, pp. 6-11; see also chapter I, p. 22.

apparently spontaneous action.[17] In *Joseph Andrews*, for example, Fielding employs this variety of denotative irony as a mock formalizing of a tavern brawl, for he uses the terminology of etiquette to describe the fight between Parson Adams and the host of the second inn. The specific denotative technique in this instance is **verbal inversion**. When, as Fielding states, the host attempted to strike Joseph,

Adams dealt him [the host] so sound a compliment over his face with his first, that the blood immediately gushed out of his nose in a stream. The host being unwilling to be outdone in courtesy, especially by a person of Adams' figure, returned the favour with so much gratitude, that the parson's nostrils began to look a little redder than usual.[18]

This same variety of denotative irony – but now as blame-by-praise, employing a shift to a different denotation – appears in *Jonathan Wild* when Fielding relates the manner of Wild's capture and subsequent imprisonment. In this instance, the formalizing is simply another means of giving to the arch criminal that mock dignity that lies behind much of the satire of the novel. Newgate becomes a castle, more "suitable" for a person of Wild's "greatness" than a prison, while the description of the incarceration relies upon terms more appropriate to a chivalric adventure.

This Law [i.e., liberty] had been promulgated a very little Time, when Mr. *Wild*, having received from some dutiful Members of the Gang, a valuable Piece of Goods, did, for a Consideration somewhat short of its original Price, re-convey it to the right Owner; for which Fact being ungratefully informed against by the said Owner, he was surprized in his own House, and being overpower'd by Numbers, was hurried before a Magistrate, and by him committed to that *Castle*, which, suitable as it is to GREATNESS, we do not chuse to name too often in our History, and where many *GREAT MEN,* at this Time, happened to be assembled.

The Governor, or as the Law more honourably calls him, *Keeper of this Castle,* having been Mr. *Wild's* old Friend and Acquaintance, made the latter greatly satisfied with the Place of his Confinement, as he promised himself not only a kind Reception and handsome

17   Humphreys, "Fielding's Irony", pp. 19-20.
18   P. 107 (II, v).

Accommodation there, but even to obtain his Liberty from him, if he thought it necessary to desire it: But alas! he was deceived, his old Friend knew him no longer, and refusing to see him, ordered the *Lieutenant Governor* to insist on as high Garnish for Fetters, and as exorbitant a Price for Lodging, as if he had had a fine Gentleman in Custody for Murther, or as if he had received an Intimation from a certain Place to use all the Severity imaginable to his Prisoner.[19]

B.   CONNOTATIVE IRONY

Connotative Irony is a much subtler device than denotative, for here Fielding depends on the connotations to make the use of a particular word ironic. Although the denotation of the word is valid in the immediate context in which it appears, its connotations are comically inappropriate. The irony arises out of this modification of the denotation by the connotations. Although there is no evidence that 18th-century writers ever employed the term *irony* with this contextual meaning in mind, Martin Price has demonstrated that Swift not only used this technique – which Mr. Price calls irony through "redefinition" – but relied on it rather heavily to achieve some of his best satiric effects.[20]

What is, of course, essential to an understanding of how connotative irony operates is our awareness that an 18th-century reader would respond to certain words much differently than would his modern counterpart, for many words in use today have lost some of the connotations they had in the 18th century. No perceptive 18th-century reader of Swift or Fielding, for example, would accept on face value such words as "modern, modest, great" or "fine gentleman". Indeed, such words had become almost ironic commonplaces in prose satire by mid-century and would almost invariably function as satiric signposts. Fielding's own ironic "Modern Glossary" provides striking illustration of how certain words could be understood when they appeared in his works. And

[19]   Henry Fielding, *Jonathan Wild*, 1743 edition (London, 1951), pp. 187-8.
[20]   Price, pp. 22-27; see also chapter I, pp. 22-23. Miss Hutchens (see note 1 above) has described essentially the same technique in *Tom Jones*, but has – more aptly, perhaps – called it "connotative irony".

of course the first edition of Johnson's *Dictionary* provides further
evidence of connotative values peculiar to the 18th century. "Miss",
for example, had pejorative as well as complimentary connotations,
for in addition to being "a Term of Honour to a young Girl", it
could also refer to "a Strumpet; a Concubine; a Whore; a Prostitute". And "modernism", a word that Johnson claimed was invented by Swift, had pejorative connotations of a different kind,
for although it denoted a "Deviation from the ancient and classical
Manner", it connoted writing that was vulgar, mean or scurrilous.
The perception of the irony inherent in the connotations of certain
words depends, therefore, on the modern reader's awareness of
these differences in usage.

In his early works, Fielding employs connotative irony in two
ways: In the first, the connotations are complimentary but contrary to what the reader knows, through the context, to be true. This
is essentially a blame-by-praise technique. The second type, however, is unique to Fielding's techniques since it employs blame
without praise. The denotation says one thing, the connotations
imply a quite different meaning, not necessarily antithetical but
invariably uncomplimentary. In both cases, however, the irony
results from a tension that is established between the context, the
denotation, and the word's connotations.

In contrast to his practice in *Tom Jones*, where connotative
irony reflects both the major themes in the novel as well as that
particular ambivalence in which something can be true in one
sense and false in another,[21] his earlier use of the technique has a
less precise focus: it is simply one of many tools of satire. For
example, connotative irony employing complimentary connotations
provides a deft touch in the characterization of a very minor figure
in *Joseph Andrews*, the mistress of the inn in Book III from which
Fanny was kidnapped by the Squire's captain. Peter Pounce has
just rescued Fanny and has returned with her to the inn.

The host, who well knew Mr. Pounce, and Lady Booby's livery, was
not a little surprised at this change of the scene: nor was his confusion
much helped by his wife, who was just now risen, and having heard
from him the account of what had passed, comforted him with a

[21]   Hutchens, "Verbal Irony", p. 47.

decent number of fools and blockheads; asked him why he did not consult her; and told him, he would never leave following the nonsensical dictates of his own numbskull, till she and her family were ruined.[22]

In this context, "decent", although denotatively valid as a purely quantitative measurement, has connotations which suggest a decorum that is comically inappropriate to this carping, shrewish innkeeper's wife.

Part of Fielding's characterization of the Tow-wouses in Book I is also dependent on connotative irony with complimentary connotations. After describing the refusal of the acrimonious Mrs. Towwouse to allow Betty or Mr. Tow-wouse to assist the injured Joseph, her browbeating of her docile husband, and his inability to interrupt her harangue with little more than a few feeble protests, Fielding tells us that "with such like *discourses* they consumed near half an hour". The "discourse" is worth quoting in its entirety for the sake of the context.

As soon as he [Mr. Tow-wouse] came in, she thus began: "What the devil do you mean by this, Mr. Tow-wouse? Am I to buy shirts to lend to a set of scabby rascals?" – "My dear," said Mr. Tow-wouse, "this is a poor wretch." – "Yes," says she, "I know it is a poor wretch; but what the devil have we to do with poor wretches? The law makes us provide for too many already. We shall have thirty or forty poor wretches in red coats shortly." – "My dear," cries Tow-wouse, "this man hath been robbed of all he hath." – "Well then", says she, "where's his money to pay his reckoning? Why doth not such a fellow go to an ale-house? I shall send him packing as soon as I am up, I assure you." – "My dear," said he, "common charity won't suffer you to do that." "Common charity, a f–t!" says she; "common charity teaches us to provide for ourselves, and our families; and I and mine won't be ruin'd by your charity, I assure you." – "Well," says he, "my dear, do as you will, when you are up; you know I never contradict you." – "No," says she, "if the devil was to contradict me, I would make the house too hot to hold him."

With such like discourses they consumed near half an hour, whilst Betty provided a shirt from the hostler, who was one of her sweethearts, and put it on poor Joseph.[23]

---

22   P. 265 (III, xii).
23   Pp. 41-2 (I, xii).

There is no question that "discourses" is literally applicable here, for at the very least this is, as Johnson defined the word, "mutual Intercourse of Language", but hardly what Johnson also referred to (connotatively) as an "Act of Understanding, by which it passes from Premises to Consequences".

Fielding uses uncomplimentary connotations as part of his characterization of Lady Booby. In dramatic contrast to her sensuousness in the seduction scenes is the suggestion of her loveless and barren marriage with Sir Thomas. Fielding touches just briefly upon this idea – first in Joseph's letter to Pamela (I, vi) and later in her revealing conversation with Slipslop in Book IV (IV, vi). When, in this latter scene, she feels compelled to defend herself against any suspicions that her scheming with Lawyer Scout may have aroused, she indignantly asks Slipslop:

"Would you insinuate that I employed Scout against this wench on the account of the fellow?" [i.e., Joseph] – "La, ma'm," said Slipslop, frighted out of her wits, "I assassinate such a thing!" "I think you dare not," answered the lady; "I believe my conduct may defy malice itself to assert so cursed a slander. If I had ever discovered any wantonness, any lightness in my behaviour: if I had followed the example of some whom thou hast, I believe, seen, in allowing myself indecent liberties, even with a husband; but the dear man who is gone" (here she began to sob), "was he alive again" (then she *produced* tears), "could not upbraid me with any one act of tenderness or passion." [24]

Although literally applicable, the coldly mechanical connotations of "produced" contradict both the actual sobbing and the emotional connotations we might ordinarily associate with weeping over the memory of a dead husband. The unintentional irony of Lady Booby's subsequent boast that in "all the time I cohabited with him, he never obtained even a kiss from me without my expressing reluctance in the granting it" [25] not only reinforces the hypocrisy of mechanically "produced" tears but exposes her typically "modern" attitude toward marriage – a reluctant cohabitation characterized by neither tenderness nor passion, a relationship in perfect accord with

[24]   Pp. 294-5 (IV, vi).
[25]   P. 295 (IV, vi).

Fielding's definitions of "love" and "marriage" in his ironic "Modern Glossary":

LOVE. A Word properly applied to our Delight in particular Kinds of Food; sometimes metaphorically spoken of the favourite Objects of all our *Appetites*.

MARRIAGE. A Kind of Traffic carried on between the two Sexes, in which both are constantly endeavouring to cheat each other, and both are commonly Losers in the End.[26]

The unemotional connotations of "produced" and "cohabited" thus betray the gravity of a scene that is intended to be a tearful remembrance of a "happily" married life, and prepare us for the final irony of Lady Booby's assertion that "I am sure he never suspected how much I loved him." [27]

C. UNDERSTATEMENT

Understatement, as Fielding uses it, is the strictly conventional technique that had been associated with irony as a rhetorical device from the late 16th century on and that was reflected in the contextual uses of the word *irony* in the 18th century,[28] as well as in modern analyses of the ironic mode in 18th-century literature. Despite this long-standing identification of understatement with rhetorical irony, however, it is important to recognize that it is quite distinct from Fielding's other techniques inasmuch as it does not function through the conventional ironic reversal or shift of meaning. With the other forms of rhetorical irony, Fielding does not mean what he says, whereas with understatement he does mean what he says but he does not say all that he means. The ironic reversal must occur, therefore, in the emphasis rather than in the meaning. Thus Fielding could be described either as "no mean satirist", or "something of a satirist".

In his early works, Fielding adopts the two forms that have been traditionally associated with understatement: litotes, where an idea

---

26   *Covent-Garden Journal*, I, p. 156.
27   P. 295 (IV, vi).
28   Knox, pp. 15-16, 78-82.

contrary to what is actually meant is denied; and meiosis, where the true meaning is belittled by an exaggerated reduction. Following his introduction of Tom Smirk in *Jonathan Wild*, Fielding uses litotes twice in ridiculing the beau as an imperfect species of the male sex:

... How must we lament that Disposition in [women] which leads them to prefer in their Favour those Individuals of the other Sex, who do not seem intended by Nature as her greatest Master-piece. For surely, however useful they may be in the Creation, as we are taught, that nothing, not even a Louse, is made in vain; yet these Beaus, even that most splendid and hounoured Part, which, in this our Island, Nature loves to distinguish in Red, are not, as some think, the noblest Part of the Creation.[29]

Meiosis is the device which Fielding employs to satirize those army officers whose motives in obtaining commissions are an abuse of their military calling. In an early issue of *The Champion* (November 27th), Fielding contrasts these men with impoverished authors and retired soldiers who had actually fought for England.

There are two sorts of persons, who may, in some sense, be said to feed on the breath which goeth out of the mouth of man; namely, the soldier and the author. But here I would not be understood to mean, by soldier, such wise military men, who justly despising this thin diet, *are content* to receive from five hundred to two thousand pounds a year, for appearing now and then in a red coat with a sash, in the parks and market-places of this kingdom, and who never saw an enemy, unless the old officers and soldiers of their own regiments, who disdain to have such commanders at their head.[30]

Not only are such "wise Military men ... *content* to receive from five hundred to two thousand pounds a year" for doing little or nothing; they are probably ecstatic.

D. REVERSAL OF STATEMENT

Fielding's Reversal of Statement is a combination of two blame-by-praise techniques implied in 18th-century contextual uses of *irony*

[29] Pp. 44-5 (I, x).
[30] *Works* (Henley), XV, p. 77.

– direct praise and Socratic self-depreciation.[31] In this case, however, as indeed with most of the techniques described below, the irony inheres in the extended statement rather than in the specific word. The ironic opening of the *Champion* for January 8th illustrates this distinction, for Fielding employs both the denotatively ironic word and, preceding it, the more inclusive reversal of statement. Just prior to an ironic diatribe against the immorality of English society, he issues this solemn promise:

> His Majesty having been pleased to set apart to-morrow as a day of solemn fast, in order to implore the blessings of Heaven on the British arms: I have thought it becoming me, as a good Englishman, to throw in my mite, and dedicate a paper to the same cause; in which *I shall cautiously avoid the least stroke of wit or humour*, it being *far* from my intention to give anything savoury to my readers on this occasion.[32]

Fielding employs this technique as either verbal inversion, as in the quotation above, or as blame-by-praise, as in the introduction to Book II of *Joseph Andrews*, where Fielding is discussing the "art" of "publishing by numbers",

> ... an art now brought to such perfection, that even dictionaries are divided and exhibited piecemeal to the public; nay, one bookseller hath ("to encourage learning and ease the public") contrived to give them a dictionary in this divided manner, *for only fifteen shillings more than it would have cost entire*.[33]

On occasion, the extended ironic statement takes the form of gratuitous advice to the reader, a technique that Reuben Brower has also identified in some of Pope's satires.[34] In Fielding's early works, this technique always appears as blame-by-praise. In *The Champion* for January 12th, for example, Fielding, posing as a defender of political apostasy, advises his readers to become turncoats whenever it seems politically advantageous for them to do so.

I know it hath been laid down, as a maxim of good policy, by one of no inconsiderable reputation, to stand firm to your principles, inas-

---

[31]   Knox, pp. 99-111.
[32]   *Works* (Henley), XV, p. 142.
[33]   P. 77 (II, i).
[34]   Brower, p. 309.

much as you may be assured that the party you adhere to will one time or other get the ascendant. But *"Vitae summa brevis, spem nos vitat inchoare longam."* Put not off until to-morrow what you can do today; you may die before you attain that by a change in the government, which you may perhaps get now by a change in your own principles.[35]

And in a later *Champion* essay (January 29th), Fielding, now posing as a worldly philosopher, advises his reader how to be an effective liar:

It will be proper always to have some regard to public notoriety [;] A–gyle's valour and dignity, Ch–ld's wit, or D–ton's politeness, will not be so judiciously called in question. Such lies as these should, if possible, be avoided. But this regards only the lie scandalous; if you come to the lie panegyrical you need set no bounds.

> "It matters not how false or forc'd,
> So the best things be said o' th' worst."

Here the assent of the world is of no consequence to you; your patron believes himself, and that is sufficient. You may lay on honour and beauty, and all manner of virtues as thick as you please, you are not to consider what he is, but what he should be, or what he would be thought. Those are the perfections you are to compliment him with, and you will scarce ever fail of success.[36]

On occasion, the reversal of statement assumes the form of an ironic concession, essentially the same technique implied in the contextual uses of the word *irony* [37] and employed by other 18th-century ironists.[38] This is simply a form of blame-by-praise in which Fielding pretends to concede the validity of a statement or position which, in actuality, he deplores. Thus, in attacking the quack doctor who, in the first book of *Joseph Andrews*, attended the wounded Joseph, Fielding ironically concedes that the doctor's "soporiferous draught" was indeed responsible for Joseph's remarkable recovery.

Joseph was now ready to sit down to a loin of mutton, and waited for Mr. Adams, when he and the doctor came in. The doctor having felt

[35]   *Works* (Henley), XV, p. 152.
[36]   *Ibid.*, pp. 173-4.
[37]   Knox, pp. 111-115.
[38]   See, for example, Pope's use of the technique in Brower, p. 251.

his pulse, and examined his wounds, declared him much better, which he imputed to that sanative soporiferous draught, a medicine "whose virtues," he said, "were never to be sufficiently extolled." *And great indeed they must be*, if Joseph was so much debted to them as the doctor imagined; since nothing more than those effluvia, which escaped the cork, could have contributed to his recovery; for the medicine had stood untouched in the window ever since its arrival.[39]

E. IRONY BY IMPLICATION

Irony by Implication, like the various types of denotative irony, is a striking example of Fielding's ability to weave subtle variations around a basically simple pattern to achieve greater stylistic variety and flexibility. With this technique, Fielding modifies the ironic statement in two ways: first, by subtly shifting the ironic point of view from the statement to the implied premise upon which it depends; second, by establishing between the two a specific logical relationship in which the statement always appears as a corollary to the implied premise. The reversal, of course, must occur in the false premise rather than in the statement which, by itself, is not ironic.

Fielding uses this technique in the early works as blame-by-praise, praise-by-blame, and as straight ironic inversion. It appears as blame-by-praise in the conclusion to the ironic dedication to Dr. John Misaubin of *The Mock Doctor*, where Fielding implies that the foolish physician is a noble and worthy gentleman – one to whom is due the highest respect for his achievements as a distinguished man of science.

And now, Sir, give me leave to conclude by wishing, that you may meet with the reward you merit: that the gratitude of some of your patients may, in return for the lengthening of their lives, contribute to immortalize your reputation; that I may see a statue erected to your memory with that serpent of Aesculapius in your hand, which you so deservedly bear in your arms, is the sincere wish of

Sir,

Your most obedient,

Most humble servant.[40]

[39] P. 64 (I, xvi).
[40] *Works* (Henley), X, p. 138.

Fielding uses this technique as praise-by-blame in one of the ironic *Champion* letters attacking virtue (January 29th), where he implies that modesty is a fault that should be avoided if a man is to achieve greatness. He advises his reader that "particular care should be taken to keep him out of the way of all manner of learning, which hath been found too apt to render men modest".[41]

Finally, irony by implication through inversion appears in the "Preface" to *Tom Thumb*, where Fielding implies (through Scriblerus) that the *Tragedy of Tragedies* is not a burlesque:

But, notwithstanding that applause which it received from all the best judges, it was severely censured by some few bad ones, and, I believe, rather maliciously than ignorantly, reported to have been intended a burlesque on the loftiest parts of tragedy, and designed to banish what we generally call fine things from the stage.[42]

F. IRONIC UNDERCUT

Fielding's Ironic Undercut is closely related in form to the ironic use of zeugma – so favored by Pope – and to what Rebecca Parkin has called the "irony of false equation",[43] for these techniques rely for their effects on an extended time lag (greater than we normally expect in irony), combined with a reversal that is not simply unexpected but shocking. It also resembles, at least in part, one of the techniques implied in 18th-century contextual uses of *irony* as blame-by-praise – Socratic self-depreciation – for it depends upon a pose that can be – though not necessarily – self-depreciatory. The ironic undercut was clearly one of Swift's most effective ironic devices [44] – although it was never identified as such by his contem-

---

[41] *Works* (Henley), XV, p. 175.
[42] *Works* (Henley), IX, p. 8.
[43] See chapter I, p. 25.
[44] See, for example, Swift's devastating attack on the Earl of Wharton in *The Examiner*. On January 4, 1710 (No. 22), Swift accused Wharton of defiling the altar at Gloucester Cathedral by doing "that which in cleanly phrase is called disburthening of Nature ...". In a subsequent issue (No. 24, January 18, 1710), Swift apologized for the accusation: "Being resolv'd publicly to confess my Mistakes I have been guilty of, I do here humbly

poraries, nor was it ever implicit, as such, in the various uses of the word *irony* in the 18th century.[45]

When he employs the ironic undercut in his early works, Fielding combines a false pose with a word or phrase which severely modifies the pose and exposes it as irony. The reader is unaware of the deception until the sudden and unexpected intrusion of the undercutting statement – a deliberately-planted signal to warn the reader that what has preceded is false. The irony, then, lies not in the inclusion of the signal but in the subsequent reversal of the preceding pose. The greater time lag here between the ironist's statement and the reader's recognition is, of course, the result of this delayed reversal. It is as if the reader were to examine casually along its entire length what appears to be a harmless red stick; only when he reaches the end does he become aware that it has a fuse that is burning furiously.

In *Jonathan Wild,* the undercut is a particularly effective means of supporting the narrator's ironic praise of Wild:

In our Hero there was nothing not truly GREAT: He could, without the least Abashment, drink a Bottle with the Man who knew he had the Moment before picked his Pocket; and, when he had stript him of everything he had, never desired to do him any farther Mischief; for he carried Good-nature to that wonderful and uncommon Height, that he never did a single Injury to Man or Woman, *by which he himself did not expect to reap some Advantage.*[46]

And in *Joseph Andrews,* the undercut functions as the ironic climax to Fielding's description of Mrs. Tow-wouse, raising to the level of comedy what would otherwise have been a brutal Hogarthian caricature.

---

desire the Reader's Pardon for one of mighty Importance, about a Fact in one of my Papers said to be done in the Cathedral of Gloucester. A whole Hydra of Errors in two Words: For as I am since inform'd, it was neither in the Cathedral, nor City, nor County of Gloucester, but some other Church of that Diocess" ([Davis], III, pp. 57 and 67-9).

[45] It seems probable that Swift's contemporaries did indeed recognize this as an ironic device but simply classified it under one of the more general techniques implied in the contextual uses of *irony.*

[46] P. 46 (I, xi).

Her person was short, thin, and crooked. Her forehead projected in the middle, and thence descended in a declivity to the top of her nose, which was sharp and red, and would have hung over her lips, had not nature turned up the end of it. Her lips were two bits of skin, which, whenever she spoke, she drew together in a purse. Her chin was peaked; and at the upper end of that skin, which composed her cheeks, stood two bones, that almost hid a pair of small red eyes. Add to this a voice most wonderfully adapted to the sentiments it was to convey, being both loud and hoarse.[47]

G. IRONIC DEFENSE

Although Fielding's Ironic Defense resembles in part the technique of the same name that was implied in the contextual uses of *irony* in the 18th century,[48] it has a much greater affinity to the type of ironic defense that modern critics have isolated as one of the salient features of Swift's satire.[49] Both writers employ this technique either as a series of statements (which can be true, partly true, false, or ambivalent) made in support of an ironic premise, or a deliberate perversion of a formal rhetorical pattern.[50] As with the undercut, the ironic defense depends to some extent on an extended time lag for its effect, for the irony of Fielding's initial premise becomes evident as the statements of "defense" become more and more patently ridiculous.

The simplest form of the ironic defense in Fielding's early works is the attribution of a false motive to an individual or institution. This is Fielding's primary mode of attacking the government in an early *Champion* paper (December 4th) in which he mockingly praises the administration's treatment of booksellers and defends censorship of the press. He assumes the pose here of Captain Vinegar's anxious bookseller, who refers to himself throughout in the third person.

He *farther begs leave (as an encouragement) to represent to you the great lenity of the administration, who have never punished any libels*

---

[47]   P. 47 (I, xiv).
[48]   Knox, pp. 119-123.
[49]   See chapter I, p. 24-25.
[50]   Bullitt, chapter III ("The Rhetoric of Satire").

against them, unless by breaking the press to pieces, pillory, fine, and imprisonment; the three last of which he apprehends to be very lawful methods, and (one of them at least) invented, as he conceives, for the benefit and advantage of booksellers, whose copies never fail to sell well, when they have been advertised in the pillory; and he would be very sorry it could with probability be insinuated among those of his profession, that he stood in any fear thereof, or ashamed to follow the steps of those glorious heroes, whose works have been published in that manner.[51]

It is for this reason that the writer begs Captain Vinegar to "infuse gall in your ink, and, instead of morality, wit, and humour, deal forth private slander and abuse . . ." so that he, the bookseller, may stand a better chance of being pilloried by the "lenient" administration.

For his description of the thief's escape in Book I of *Joseph Andrews*, Fielding employs a series of false motives:

Barnabas and the surgeon being returned, as we have said, to the inn, in order to convey the thief before the justice, were greatly concerned to find a small accident had happened, which somewhat disconcerted them; and this was no other than the thief's escape, who had *modestly* withdrawn himself by night, *declining all ostentation, and not choosing, in imitation of some great men, to distinguish himself at the expense of being pointed at.*[52]

Continuing the irony of "modestly", Fielding gives as the motives for the thief's escape: shyness, modesty, a desire to avoid notoriety – motives which are not simply and blatantly false but which make of the thief – who had beaten, robbed, and stripped poor Joseph and left him for dead on the road at night – a minor mock hero, possessing the very virtues of his victim.

A more extended form of the ironic defense is the relatively straightforward presentation of evidence (opinions, truisms, empirical observations) supporting an ironic premise. There is no formal rhetorical pattern imposed on the defense, nor is there usually much, if any, exaggeration. The whole trick is to make it sound perfectly reasonable, perfectly obvious. The ironic distortion,

---

[51]   *Works* (Henley), XV, p. 84; the italics are Fielding's.
[52]   P. 56 (I, xvi).

carefully underplayed, lies in the subtle manipulation and deliberate misinterpretation of the evidence. Thus, in the *Champion* for February 5th, Fielding (again as Captain Vinegar) glibly supports the ironic premise that "very good effects" result from the presence of a scolding woman in a house.

> For my own part, I cannot help thinking that several very good effects are produced from this practice. My wife Joan tells me, that, on going into any family, we may easily see, by the regularity and order of affairs, whether the mistress of the house be a scold or not; to which perhaps the old adage concerning the best mustard may allude.
> A very ingenious clergyman of the Church of *England* hath assured me, that he found a very sensible alteration (for the better) in his parishioners, upon the settlement of a very excellent scold among them. Whatever vice or enormity any in the parish were guilty of, they were very sure of hearing it, as the proverb says, "On both sides of their ears," by this good woman; who, the doctor very pleasantly assured me, did more towards the preservation of good manners by these daily lectures which she exhibited gratis in the streets, than he could by all his sermons in the pulpit.
> I believe, it hath been often found, that men, whom the preservation of their healths and fortunes, nay, even the very terror of the laws could not restrain from extravagancy, have owed their reformation to a curtain-lecture. I do remember, when I was a young fellow, to have heard a man excuse himself for retiring early from his debauched companions, by saying, "Gentlemen, you know I have a wife at home."
> Nor is this practice as it hath been represented, confined within the precincts of Billingsgate, or the lower orb of people only. There are scolds of all ranks and degrees, and I have known a Right Honourable, who could be heard all over a large palace to her praise with great facility.[53]

When the statements of support are placed within a pseudo-rhetorical framework where the intention is to convince by an extended logical progression instead of by the mere accumulation of evidence, the technique then becomes the *reductio ad absurdum*, a rhetorical device commonly associated with irony in the 18th century. (The association, however, was through burlesque, as Professor Knox has shown, for the word *irony* was often used to cover a series of techniques – the *reductio ad absurdum* among

---

[53]   *Works* (Henley), XV, pp. 183-4.

them – that were really types of burlesque.[54]) In Book II of *Joseph
Andrews*, for example, Fielding uses the *reductio* to inject into the
description of the mock battle between Parson Adams and Fanny's
would-be ravisher the same note of mock seriousness that characterizes every one of the fights in *Joseph Andrews*. As Adams
swings his staff at the head of Fanny's attacker, Fielding stops the
action and embarks on a lengthy defense of the premise that nature protects the ignorant in this world by providing them with
extra-thick skulls to occupy the space ordinarily filled by brains.

> ... Lifting up his crabstick, [Adams] immediately levelled a blow at
> that part of the ravisher's head, where, according to the opinion of
> the ancients, the brains of some persons are deposited, and which he
> had undoubtedly let forth, had not Nature (who, as wise men have
> observed, equips all creatures with what is most expedient for them)
> taken a provident care (as she always doth with those she intends for
> encounters) to make this part of the head three times as thick as
> those of ordinary men, who are designed to exercise talents which are
> vulgarly called rational, and for whom, as brains are necessary, she is
> obliged to leave some room for them in the cavity of the skull;
> whereas, those ingredients being entirely useless to persons of the
> heroic calling, she hath an opportunity of thickening the bone, so as
> to make it less subject to any impression, or liable to be cracked or
> broken; and indeed, in some who are predestined to the command of
> armies and empires, she is supposed sometimes to make that part
> perfectly solid.[55]

Fielding begins by ridiculing fighters or soldiers only – those whom
nature "intends for encounters" – but he is soon directing his ironic
barbs at more distinguished thick-skulls. Thus not only does the
argument develop – through a kind of twisted logic – from an absurd

---

[54] Knox, pp. 125-135. Fielding, however, never used the word *irony* in
this manner. According to Richmond P. Bond, burlesque, formally defined,
was the imitation of serious or trivial matter in an incongruous manner
(*English Burlesque Poetry: 1700-1750*, Cambridge, 1932, p. 3; see also
chapter III). Fielding's understanding of the term, as it can be inferred
from the Preface to *Joseph Andrews*, seems to be no more than that. It is
not improbable, however, that he was conscious of this extended meaning
of *irony*. His awareness that he had used a device that could be classified
as burlesque by some critics might serve to explain in part his sensitivity
to the possible accusation that he had written a burlesque rather than a
comic work.
[55] Pp. 126-7 (II, ix).

premise to an even more absurd conclusion, but it also proceeds through a kind of social hierarchy: from the obscure ravisher of a helpless girl, to soldiers, to generals, to ruling ministers or kings – ravishers all. The final implication is clear: the higher one rises in this hierarchy, the less need "to exercise talents which are vulgarly called rational".

For his other major type of ironic defense, Fielding again follows rhetorical tradition by employing distortions of two conventional modes of argumentation – the syllogism and the analogy.[56] Thus, in the *Champion* for April 22nd, Fielding ironically defends the style of Cibber's *Apology* with two consecutive false syllogisms:

Now I shall prove it to be English in the following manner. Whatever book is writ in no other language, is writ in English. This book is writ in no other language, *ergo*, It is writ in English: Of which language the author has shown himself a most absolute master; for surely he must be absolute master of that whose laws he can trample under feet, and which he can use as he pleases.[57]

And in the ironic essay on turncoats (January 12th), Fielding defends political apostasy with a false analogy. In defending the supposed etymology of the word *turncoat,* he points out that it is

a compound word, intended to express what we generally call good housewifery. The Turn-coats were no others than certain prudent persons, who, as soon as their coat was sufficiently soiled on one side, were wont to order it to the right about, and make a very handsome and decent figure with the other side.

Hence this term became afterwards metaphorically applied to those gentlemen, who, perhaps, from much the same reasons, turned from one party to the other; changing their opinions, as the other did their coats, to the very reverse of what they formerly were.[58]

In general, these techniques of verbal irony, considered collectively, constitute a major vehicle for the comedy of Fielding's early works, for it is verbal irony that helps establish the tone of the comic

[56] See Bullitt on the spurious enthymeme (pp. 112-122) and the example (pp. 82-92) for a discussion of Swift's use of these devices. See also Knox, pp. 123-125; and Leavis, "The Irony of Swift", p. 370.
[57] *Works* (Henley), XV, p. 291.
[58] *Ibid.*, p. 150.

prose prefaces to the plays and of the comic essays of *The Champion*; and it is verbal irony that becomes a major means of developing both the satiric characterizations and thematic contrasts upon which much of the comedy of *Joseph Andrews* depends. More specifically, verbal irony in these works becomes a means of establishing the distance between the object and the reader that is so essential to comedy. Through this distancing, verbal irony helps diminish, in effect, both the size of any object and the gravity of any situation. (In this respect, the effects of irony and burlesque coincide; the difference lies only in the means to the effect.) It becomes an invisible barrier – or, more properly, perhaps, a reversed telescope – that is placed between the object and both the sympathy and empathy of the reader. Thus in the scene from *Joseph Andrews* described above, where Parson Adams rescues Fanny, it is verbal irony that diminishes not only the seriousness of the struggle between Adams and the would-be ravisher and the possibility (actually, as it turns out, the *im*possibility) of a cracked skull,[59] but – through an ironic simile – reduces the entire scene to nothing larger than a squabble between two game cocks over a hen. Immediately following the ironic defense of thick-skulls, Fielding adds:

As a game cock, when engaged in amorous toying with a hen, if perchance he espies another cock at hand, immediately quits his female, and opposes himself to his rival; so did the ravisher, on the information of the crabstick, immediately leap from the woman, and hasten to assail the man.[60]

The irony, and ultimately the comedy, of the scene as a whole is, of course, intensified by the flippant reference to Adams as just "another cock".

When the intention behind such distancing is satire – as it almost always is when Fielding employs these techniques as a means of characterization – then verbal irony becomes to Fielding what the various other techniques of satire were to his Augustan contemporaries – a shield of good form which conceals the satirist's real

---

[59]   See p. 86.
[60]   P. 127 (II, ix).

emotions. Irony becomes an indirect means of expressing the satirist's rage, his disgust, his hatred without paying the price – without violating the decorum of an age that deplored not simply the overt expression of such feelings but any kind of emotional gaucherie. Outright laughter must be compressed into the carefully cultivated smile that contains within itself infinite subtleties and complexities. As Lord Chesterfield advised his son,

> Having mentioned laughing, I must particularly warn you against it: and I could heartily wish that you may often be seen to smile, but never heard to laugh while you live. Frequent and loud laughter is the characteristic of folly and ill manners: it is the manner in which the mob express their silly joy at silly things; and they call it being merry. In my mind, there is nothing so illiberal and so ill bred, as audible [sic] laughter. . . . I am neither of a melancholy nor a cynical disposition, and am as willing, and as apt, to be pleased as anybody; but I am sure that, since I had the full use of reason, nobody has ever heard me laugh.[61]

Verbal irony, like the flickering smile, then, becomes a measure of Fielding's control as a comic artist, a test, a challenge – in much the same way that the heroic couplet was a test of Pope's control as a poet. The more carefully cultivated, the more subtle the irony, the more appropriate the manner, the greater the distance between the printed page and the confluence of thought and feeling that prompted it.

Quite apart from the aesthetic and psychological necessity for such distancing, there is a more general moral purpose in much of the verbal irony in these early works, for quite often it serves to point up the dangers of acquiescing too readily in the separation of language from reality. This is, of course, the semantic equivalent of faith without good works, which to Fielding was sheer hypocrisy. Thus, to call the physician who treated Joseph in Book I of *Joseph Andrews* "learned" may well lead to both the comic and satiric exposure of the man, but the ironic reference also has moral implications inasmuch as it emphasizes how far his "professing" is inconsistent with his profession. And to praise ironically Leonora's Aunt in *Joseph Andrews* for her "Christian forgiveness" (II, iv) is

---

[61] *Letters*, III, pp. 1115-1116 (Mar. 9, 1748).

to show the extent to which the aunt is willing to allow the nominal to stand for the real. Perhaps the extreme illustrations of such separation of words from reality are Fielding's later ironic definitions of "love" and "marriage" that I quoted at the beginning of this chapter. When such words become meaningless, they cannot help but affect the things they represent. Verbal irony thus becomes a means of constantly holding up before us the importance of recognizing that words have real consequences in the real world.

These various functions of verbal irony, as well as its subtlety and complexity, become increasingly apparent in Fielding's early works as he progresses from playwright to journalist to novelist. Whereas in the prefaces to the plays, he uses only two relatively unsophisticated techniques (denotative irony as blame-by-praise with antithetical denotations, and the simplest form of reversal of statement), in *Joseph Andrews* he employs frequently every one of the verbal devices described in this chapter. (The frequency with which Fielding used specific techniques will be discussed more fully in the conclusion.) There seems little doubt that by the time the playwright-journalist turned to the novel, he had become aware of the possibilities that verbal irony presented to him. And the best of these possibilities was, as the following chapter will, I hope, demonstrate, the application of these verbal techniques to satiric characterization.

IV

RHETORICAL IRONY
III: VERBAL IRONY IN *JOSEPH ANDREWS*

Joseph Andrews provides the best example of how these techniques of verbal irony function collectively as a mode of comedy,
for nowhere else in his early works does Fielding employ them as
frequently and with as much subtlety. In this novel, Fielding uses
verbal irony primarily as a vehicle for satiric characterization, and,
to a lesser degree, both as a structural support for the various
thematic patterns that are woven into the finely textured fabric of
Joseph Andrews, and as a means of focusing on the parody that is
potentially present in most of the highly stylized scenes. These
various functions, however, should not be considered mutually
exclusive, for, as I shall attempt to show, they frequently comple-
ment one another rather closely.

What is unique to Fielding is the successful application on a
relatively large scale of a popular rhetorical mode to fictional characterization. He had tried it earlier with *Jonathan Wild*, but as I
shall show in the conclusion, the irony of that novel seldom, if
ever, matches the variety or the sophistication of the irony in *Joseph
Andrews*. Consequently, we find that verbal irony figures significantly in the portraits of those people who are satirized most heavily – Slipslop, Lady Booby, and Beau Didapper, among others. It
should be apparent, however, that irony is not the only mode
through which Fielding characterizes the many comic and grotesque people who waddle, strut, and wheedle their way through the
pages of this engaging narrative, for his experience as a dramatist
made him as conscious of the many ways of allowing characters to
expose themselves as he was of the subtleties of the authorial intrusion. In this novel, style becomes as great an achievement as narra-

tive control – a style whose deft, ironic touches add to the portraits of Lady Booby, Slipslop, Beau Didapper, and others subtle nuances of character that enable us to see these people most clearly at the peak of their absurdity.

Fielding's treatment of Slipslop, the lustful but "prudent" chambermaid to the Lady Booby, provides perhaps the most compelling illustration of the combined effect of these techniques for characterization. When the corpulent Slipslop waddles her way into Fielding's narrative, it signifies the commencement of the most persistent ironic attack made on any single character in the novel. The result is a lengthy characterization that bears out the promise of the initial description of Slipslop's person in I, vi.

If we were to take Fielding's words literally, Slipslop would be the most attractive person in *Joseph Andrews*. She would be a gentlewoman of impeccable morality; she would possess the Christian virtues; she would be reasonable, philosophical, courteous, and would display great prudence, particularly in emotionally intricate situations. Despite her insistence upon an impregnable chastity, she could be tender when the occasion warranted it and even sexually alluring. She would also be fair, charming, faithful, and of a tranquil disposition. The reader does not have to progress much beyond the first few lines of Fielding's introduction of Slipslop to perceive the transparency of his irony. Yet these are the qualities Fielding attributes to her throughout – but never, it should be added, in such a manner as to require only a simple reversal of meaning.

In his first reference to Slipslop (the title to I, iii), Fielding calls her, and quite correctly, "the chambermaid". This term is never used again to describe her, yet it is the only one of the several titles associated with Slipslop that is both denotatively and connotatively true. She is chambermaid to the Lady Booby and nothing more. The term that takes its place in almost every important scene in which she appears and which is used almost exclusively with Slipslop is "gentlewoman", which, although denotatively appropriate, has connotatively ironic overtones that tend to highlight the affectations of a socially pretentious chambermaid.[1] But even more im-

[1]   As Dr. Johnson noted, the word could refer to a woman "who waits

portant, these ironic references to Slipslop's gentility reinforce one
of the major thematic contrasts of the book, that between nominal
and genuine gentility (or nobility), for all of the major and many of
the minor characters in *Joseph Andrews* polarize around one or
the other of these points and this polarization in turn becomes one
means of measuring character. It is through Slipslop that Fielding
introduces this thematic contrast and keeps it before us when she
is with Lady Booby in particular, for only when we see what she
really aspires to – as embodied in Lady Booby – can we fully ap-
preciate the absurdity of her social pretensions.

When he introduces Slipslop, Fielding employs the undercut to
intensify the irony of negative understatement. Together, these
devices emphasize two elements in particular – Slipslop's looks and
her attempts to win Joseph's favor – both significant, as will be
seen, in determining her relationship to Fanny, with whom she is
constantly (if implicitly) contrasted.

She was not at this time remarkably handsome; being very short, and
rather too corpulent in body, and somewhat red, with the addition of
pimples in the face. Her nose was likewise rather too large, and her
eyes too little; nor did she resemble a cow so much in her breath, as
in two brown globes which she carried before her; one of her legs was

---

about the person of one of high Rank"; and in "An Essay on Conversation", Fielding used the term to suggest a lady of genteel manner and bear-
ing (*Works* [Henley], XIV, p. 266). To an 18th-century reader, therefore,
the connotations ordinarily evoked by "gentlewoman" would clash sharply
with what he already knows to be true about Lady Booby's chambermaid.
The possibility too that an 18th-century reader would recognize the irony
more immediately than a modern reader is suggested quite strongly by
Johnson's added observations that "gentlewoman" was also employed "as a
word of civility or irony". Finally, Fielding's avoidance of the term in
describing Sophia's chambermaid in *Tom Jones* confirms his ironic-satiric
intention here. Honour is no less affected or socially pretentious than Slipslop, yet Fielding, with but a single exception, never refers to her as anything but "waiting-woman", a title having the same general connotations as
"chambermaid" according to Johnson. Honour, to be sure, is relatively
colorless when placed beside Slipslop, but might not this be a result of
Fielding's avoidance of such connotative distinctions whenever Honour
does appear in the novel? Furthermore, the only time Fielding does call
Honour a "gentlewoman" (X, iv) is when he wants deliberately to ridicule
her social affectations. As with Slipslop, the connotations of "gentlewoman"
emphasize what Honour would like to be considered but is not.

also a little shorter than the other, which occasioned her to limp as she walked. This fair creature had long cast the eyes of affection on Joseph, in which she had not met with quite so good success as she probably wished. . . .[2]

In subsequent descriptions, denotatively ironic references to Slipslop's "good" looks and connotatively ironic references to her prudence, chastity, amorousness, and intelligence help to sustain throughout *Joseph Andrews* the Hogarthian flavor of this introductory picture.

Aside from her lust for Joseph, the chief motives for most of Slipslop's actions in *Joseph Andrews* are a rapacious self-interest and an obsession with a reputation for chastity. In certain respects, she is shrewd and she is constantly conniving to manipulate things to her own advantage in the Booby household. A means of focusing our attention on these characteristics in particular are Fielding's frequent connotatively ironic references to Slipslop's "prudence", a word whose usual connotative values are inapplicable here. (His method here should be contrasted to his infinitely more sophisticated use of "prudence" in *Tom Jones* [3] where it becomes considerably more than a means of ironic focus.)

To an 18th-century reader, "prudence" would most immediately connote an ethical quality. Exhortations to prudence specifically as a rule of conduct were quite common in 18th-century didactic fiction,[4] and Samuel Johnson's primary definitions of the term suggest similarly ethical connotations – sound judgment, wisdom, perception. These positive connotations of "prudence" are further supported by its contextual appearances in the works of Fielding's contemporaries [5] as well as in his own earlier works, where it was synonymous with "wisdom".[6] On the other hand, the application of

[2]   P. 16 (I, vi).
[3]   See Maurice Johnson, *Fielding's Art of Fiction* (Philadelphia, 1961), pp. 115-119, and Eleanor N. Hutchens, "Prudence in *Tom Jones*", *PQ*, XXXIX (October, 1960), pp. 496-507.
[4]   Johnson, *Fielding's Art of Fiction*, pp. 116-117.
[5]   See, for example, Swift's use of "prudence" in *Gulliver's Travels*, ed. Louis Landa, Riverside edition (Boston, 1960), pp. 36 and 58.
[6]   See *The Letter-Writers* (*Works* [Henley], IX, p. 182), *The Miser* (*Works* [Henley], X, pp. 204, 230, 238), *The Intriguing Chambermaid* (*Works* [Henley], X, pp. 287, 290), *The Universal Gallant* (*Works* [Henley], XI,

"prudence" in an ironic or purely comic sense was not unique to
Joseph Andrews. In the 1744 revision of his moral essay, "Of the
Characters of Women", Pope played upon the ironic contrast between denotative and connotative values of "prudence" in the
character of Chloe.[7] And occasionally in his own plays, Fielding
employs "prudence" as a means of comic exposure.[8]

Slipslop's is a prudence lacking in any kind of moral value.
Consider, for example, Fielding's first use of the word in his description of the crisis between Lady Booby and her chambermaid,
precipitated by the latter's key-hole snooping.

She then called Slipslop up, and, after refreshing her spirits with a
small cordial, which she kept in her closet, she began in the following
manner:
"Slipslop, why will you, who know my passionate temper, attempt
to provoke me by your answers? I am convinced you are an honest
servant, and should be very unwilling to part with you. I believe,
likewise, you have found me an indulgent mistress on many occasions,
and have as little reason on your side to desire a change. I can't help
being surprised, therefore, that you will take the surest method to
offend me – I mean, repeating my words, which you know I have
always detested."
The prudent waiting-gentlewoman had duly weighed the whole
matter, and found, on mature deliberation, that a good place in pos-
session was better than one in expectation. As she found her mistress
therefore inclined to relent, she thought proper also to put on some
small condescension; which was as readily accepted; and so the affair
was reconciled, all offences forgiven, and a present of a gown and
petticoat made her, as an instance of her Lady's future favour.[9]

---

pp. 81, 87, 114, 118), *The Historical Register* (*Works* [Henley], XI, pp. 231,
266), *Eurydice Hiss'd* (*Works* [Henley], XI, p. 297), and *The Champion*,
January 12, 1739-40 (*Works* [Henley], XV, p. 150); see also Battestin, p. 45.
[7] Alexander Pope, *Epistles to Several Persons (Moral Essays)*, ed. F. W.
Bateson, Twickenham edition, III, ii (London, 1951), p. 62.
[8] For example, to Lovegold, the personification of miserliness in *The
Miser*, "prudence" means only economic soundness or financial feasibility
(*Works* [Henley], X, pp. 190, 195, 196, 201, 230, 242). And to Lady Raffler,
the self-righteous prude in *The Universal Gallant*, "prudence" is primarily
a synonym for sexual discretion (*Works* [Henley], XI, pp. 95, 133, 146).
By contrast, Fielding's ironic uses of the term in *Joseph Andrews* are placed
strictly within the context of blame-by-praise.
[9] P. 29 (I, ix).

Slipslop's is clearly a practical decision and to that degree can be described as "prudent". But we must recognize too that her prudence is severely qualified by the extent to which Lady Booby has compromised herself by underestimating her chambermaid's cunning, for Slipslop is able to make this "prudent" decision only because Lady Booby is herself *im*prudent enough to allow herself to be blackmailed. And what further modifies and deflates the ethical and moral connotations of "prudence" here is the fact that Slipslop's decision has been made in the light of some very *un*ethical eavesdropping.

Equally incongrous are Fielding's associations of "prudence" with Slipslop's exaggerated concern for her chaste reputation. When Didapper becomes aware during the nightwalking scene in Booby Hall that the woman he is attempting to rape is someone other than Fanny and tries to retreat, Slipslop holds him fast, realizing with "wonderful presence of mind" that she could use his error to her own advantage.

> For that prudent woman being disappointed of those delicious offerings which her fancy had promised her pleasure, resolved to make an immediate sacrifice to her virtue. Indeed she wanted an opportunity to heal some wounds, which her late conduct had, she feared, given her reputation, and as she had a wonderful presence of mind, she conceived the person of the unfortunate beau to be luckily thrown in her way to restore her lady's opinion of her impregnable chastity.[10]

The connotations evoked here by "prudence" as a moral virtue are particularly inappropriate when juxtaposed against Slipslop's real motive: her desire to "restore her Lady's opinion of her impregnable chastity" by claiming that Didapper had "ruined" her in her sleep.

The references to Slipslop's "chastity" provide perhaps the most striking illustrations of how Fielding employs connotative irony in *Joseph Andrews* to bring out subtleties of character. Fielding prefaces his initial description, for example, by informing us that "she was a *maiden* gentlewoman of about forty-five years of age, who having made a small slip in her youth, had continued a good *maid*

---

[10]   P. 332 (IV, xiv).

ever since" (I, vi). And in the scene in Slipslop's bedroom during
that confusing evening in Booby Hall, he speaks first of her "impregnable chastity" (see above); then of the "chaste Slipslop" (IV,
xiv). Now, "chaste" certainly has denotative validity when applied
to Slipslop. It is not difficult to see why. But the conventional
connotations of "chaste", "chastity", "maid", and "maiden" are
hardly appropriate to Slipslop. Hers is an unwilling chastity and
she does everything in her power, short of jeopardizing her reputation and her position with Lady Booby, to overcome the frustra-
tion of a lifetime of enforced abstinence.

The truth is she was arrived at an age when she thought she might
indulge herself in any liberties with a man, without the danger of
bringing a third person into the world to betray them. She imagined
that by so long a self-denial she had not only made amends for the
small slip in her youth above hinted at, but had likewise laid up a
quantity of merit to excuse any future failings. In a word, she resolved
to give a loose to her amorous inclinations, and to pay off the debt
of pleasure which she found she owed herself, as fast as possible.[11]

Opposed to Slipslop's chastity are the connotatively ironic references to her sexual allure. The ridicule of her ludicrous attempts to
put an end to her sexual frustrations by devouring the "luscious"
Joseph is only heightened by Fielding's describing her as "amorous" or "tender". And in the great bedroom scene, Fielding displays more than his usual flamboyance in ironically describing her
first as Didapper's "paramour" and then as Parson Adams's "bed-
fellow".

It is through the implicit presence of Fanny in much of what
Fielding ironically says about Slipslop, however, that the irony of
his characterization of Lady Booby's chambermaid acquires a more
subtle dimension. In almost every instance, Fielding's ironic statements about Slipslop are both denotatively and connotatively true
of Fanny who, as a foil to the grotesque Slipslop, is not only beautiful (contrast her description in II, xii) but – more significantly – is
successful in winning the virtuous Joseph. Indeed, it is Fanny, if
anybody, who is the true gentlewoman in *Joseph Andrews* and
hardly Slipslop, for as Fielding tells us later, Fanny "had a natural

[11]   P. 16 (I, vi).

gentility, superior to the acquisition of art, and which surprised all who beheld her" (II, xii). And Slipslop's lascivious maneuverings, her butchery of the English language, and her vaunted "chastity" are a constantly amusing contrast to Fanny's quiet but appealing femininity, her simple, unaffected speech, and her genuine chastity.

Employing a quite different series of ironic techniques, Fielding enables us to see how neatly Lady Booby, on the other hand, complements her chambermaid's prudence, chastity, and amorousness with a highly suspect "innocence". If the noblewoman's inflated ego is pricked by the indignity of a bedside lecture on virtue delivered to her by a common servant, the artificiality of her behavior is exposed in a number of places by Fielding's ironic comments upon the "innocence" of her motives in attempting to seduce her footman. Fielding concentrates his ironic characterization here on the seduction scenes of Book I, his descriptive touches illuminating with delightful subtlety the folly of Lady Booby's own actions.

He "conceals" her first attempts at coquetry with Joseph behind false motives, but betrays his ironic pose from the beginning by sharply undercutting the first motive.

She would now walk out with him into Hyde Park in a morning, and *when tired, which happened almost every minute*, would lean on his arm, and converse with him in great familiarity. Whenever she stept out of her coach, she would take him by the hand, and sometimes, *for fear of stumbling*, press it very hard.[12]

Her subsequent behavior is labeled with quite pointed denotative irony, "innocent freedoms".

She admitted him to deliver messages at her bedside in a morning, leered at him at table, and indulged him in all those *innocent* freedoms which women of figure may permit without the least sully of their virtue.

But whatever opinion or suspicion the scandalous inclination of defamers might entertain of Lady Booby's *innocent freedoms*, it is certain they made no impression on young Andrews. . . .[13]

And when she recoils from the shock of listening to her footman defend his virtue against her advances, she proclaims indignantly,

[12]   Pp. 10-11 (I, iv).
[13]   P. 11 (I, iv).

"Yes, sirrah, . . . you have had the vanity to misconstrue the little *innocent freedom* I took, in order to try whether what I had heard was true" (I, viii).

Fielding's ironic insistence on Lady Booby's "innocence" is maintained during his description of her second attempt to seduce Joseph, but now more implicitly.

The lady being in bed, called Joseph to her, bade him sit down, and having *accidentally* laid her hand on his, she asked him, if he had ever been in love.[14]

And on the third interview, inadvertence becomes carelessness.

"Come hither, Joseph; another mistress might discard you for these offences; but I have a compassion for your youth, and if I could be certain you would be no more guilty – Consider, child" (laying her hand *carelessly* upon his), "you are a handsome fellow and might do better; you might make your fortune." [15]

The "innocence" with which Lady Booby treats her honest footman is, as Fielding implies, not inconsistent with those things which she considers the "most valuable blessings of life". When the possibility of discharging Slipslop occurs to her, Lady Booby becomes suddenly aware of the risk involved in such an action; and once more Fielding exposes her pretensions with denotative irony.

But the dismissing of Mrs. Slipslop was a point not so easily to be resolved upon. She had the utmost tenderness for her reputation, as she knew on that depended many of the most valuable blessings of life; particularly cards, making curtsies in public places, and, above all, the pleasure of demolishing the reputations of others, in which *innocent amusement* she had an extraordinary delight. She therefore determined to submit to any insult from a servant, rather than run a risk of losing the title to so many great privileges.[16]

The reiteration of the innocence motif serves as a subtle counterpoint to the entire movement of the seduction, from Lady Booby's casual strolls in Hyde Park with her footman to her angry dismissal of Joseph. In particular, this motif helps bring into focus the

[14]   P. 12 (I, v).
[15]   Pp. 23-4 (I, viii).
[16]   P. 28 (I, ix).

nakedness theme which is announced for the first time in *Joseph Andrews* during the initial interview in Lady Booby's closet.

> She then raised herself a little in her bed, and discovered one of the whitest necks that ever was seen; at which Joseph blushed. "La!" says she, in an affected surprise, "what am I doing? I have trusted myself with a man alone, naked in bed; suppose you should have any wicked intentions upon my honour, how should I defend myself?" [17]

With the virtuous characters in *Joseph Andrews,* especially Fanny, Adams, and Joseph, nakedness is invariably associated with innocence and worth.[18] In Lady Booby, we see the converse, her nakedness representing lust, lewdness, the corrupt world of experience. With the virtuous characters, nakedness results from accident or inadvertence; with Lady Booby, it is the result of deliberate artifice. Ultimately, this contrast becomes a symbolic pattern that recurs with some frequency in *Joseph Andrews*, in which people are always being stripped, either literally (of their clothing) or figuratively (of their affectations). And this pattern, in turn, reinforces significantly several of the themes that dominate the novel: nature vs. artifice, innocence vs. corruption, charity vs. self-aggrandizement, true gentility (or nobility) vs. false. With Lady Booby in these early seduction scenes, Fielding's irony points up the deliberate reversal of these values in which her prurient self-exposure (both literal and figurative) is passed off as genuine innocence, the irony stemming from the application of the values of one type of nakedness to another.

(It is also possible that Lady Booby's pretended innocence was intended by Fielding to function as a further parody of *Pamela*, supplementing the more obvious parody present in the situation of the virtuous footman seeking to emulate the chaste behavior of his famous sister. Fielding's irony here may be a means of suggesting that false innocence masks Lady Booby's motives with the same hypocrisy that it did Pamela's.)

This ironic insistence on Lady Booby's pretended innocence

---

[17]   P. 13 (I, v).
[18]   Mark Spilka, "Comic Resolution in Fielding's *Joseph Andrews*", *College English*, XV (October, 1953), p. 14. Mr. Spilka, however, speaks of nakedness only in relation to Parson Adams.

also serves ultimately to focus on her relationship to Fanny, for, like Slipslop, Lady Booby must also be considered a foil to Joseph's demure sweetheart. The "innocent freedoms", the "accidental" situations, and the false modesty that Lady Booby assumes when she displays "one of the whitest necks that ever was seen", comprise the ironic contrast to Fanny's genuine innocence and to her modesty when, in Book IV, she too stands partially naked before the transfixed Joseph.

Fielding climaxes his ironic defense of Lady Booby's innocence by suggesting that we should not be too harsh in our judgment of her, for the temptation that was placed before her was so "vast" as to easily overcome "all the efforts of a modest and virtuous mind" (I, viii). The temptation is, of course, Joseph:

Mr. Joseph Andrews was now in the one-and-twentieth year of his age. He was of the highest degree of middle stature. His limbs were put together with great elegance, and no less strength. His legs and thighs were formed in the exactest proportion. His shoulders were broad and brawny; but yet his arms hung so easily, that he had all the symptoms of strength without the least clumsiness. His hair was of a nut-brown colour, and was displayed in wanton ringlets down his back. His forehead was high, his eyes dark, and as full of sweetness as of fire. His nose a little inclined to the Roman. His teeth white and even. His lips full, red, and soft. His beard was only rough on his chin and upper lip; but his cheeks, in which his blood glowed, were overspread with a thick down. His countenance had a tenderness joined with a sensibility inexpressible.[19]

The details of diction and phrasing suggest something considerably less than an objective portrait, for we are being treated here to a view of Joseph not as he actually is, but as seen through the glaze of sexually-starved eyes [20] – the ancient fertility god Priapus himself, transformed for the occasion into a handsome Apollo and performing now a much different "office" than that of "keeping birds" (I, ii). Slipslop, who saw Joseph with the same adoration, made what was virtually a collective slip-of-the-tongue when she

[19]   P. 23 (I, viii).
[20]   That this description was deliberately contrived is suggested by the fact that Fielding had used this device before. In his play, *An Old Man Taught Wisdom*, Miss Lucy describes the footman, Thomas, in a similar manner.

referred to Joseph earlier as "a strong, healthy, *luscious* boy . . ."
(I, vi).

Yet to this perfect picture, Fielding contributes a subtle but
jarring ironic note that further confirms Lady Booby's inability to
see more than what she really wants to see.

Add to this the most perfect neatness in his dress, and an air, which,
to those who have not seen many noblemen, would give an air of
nobility.[21]

Since Fielding has been emphasizing, through his verbal irony
primarily, both the falsity of Lady Booby's apparent motives and
the dominance of passion over her rational faculties, it is significant that he chooses to conclude his defense of the noblewoman
on a totally ambiguous note, for the undercutting phrase casts
doubt not only upon Joseph's nobility but upon the true nobility of
noblemen as well. What she *thinks* she sees is about as reliable as
what she *does* see, and primarily because Lady Booby – like those
other "fine" ladies and gentlemen upon whose good will she relies
so desperately – perceives value only through externals and such
nominal distinctions as "nobleman" and "gentlewoman". In other
words, what Joseph *is* is not any more reliable that what he *appears*
to be to Lady Booby, for not only is Joseph's nobility a point of
dispute, but so is even the larger question of the nobility of noblemen.

Fielding's ironic praise of Lady Booby's rationality in Book IV
not only focuses our attention again on the resemblance between
Lady Booby and Slipslop – a resemblance made explicit earlier by
his use of Slipslop (in I, vi) to parody Lady Booby's attempted
seduction of Joseph – but strikes again at the purely external and
essentially meaningless distinction here between these two "gentle-
women" when true gentility is absent. In Book IV, Lady Booby's
decision to give Joseph up after it seems that nothing can prevent
his marrying Fanny is simply a more sophisticated version of Slipslop's similar decision in Book I. To Lady Booby, it has finally
become quite apparent that an unblemished reputation is more

---

[21]   P. 23 (I, viii).

valuable ultimately than a "mean and vile" attempt to satisfy her sexual appetite.

> To sacrifice my reputation, my character, my rank in life, to the indulgence of a mean and vile appetite! How I detest the thought! How much more exquisite is the pleasure resulting from the reflection of virtue and prudence, than the faint relish of what flows from vice and folly! Whither did I suffer this improper, this mad passion to hurry me, only by neglecting to summon the aid of reason to my assistance? Reason, which hath now set before me my desires in their proper colors, and immediately helped me to expel them.[22]

The irony implicit here in Lady Booby's view of herself is made quite explicit by Fielding's subsequent comment on this soliloquy where he praises those "admirable reflections which the supreme power of reason had so wisely made" (IV, xiii).

What really overcomes her passion for Joseph is not reason, as she terms it, but vanity. The "pleasure" Lady Booby tries to convince herself she is experiencing is not the result of her "reflection of virtue and prudence" but her fear of losing her reputation, her character, her rank in the *beau monde*. Virtue is irrelevant; and prudence here is little more than the greater lure of reputation. That this decision is itself overturned as easily as it was made when Lady Booby decides later to marry Joseph after learning that he and Fanny are apparently brother and sister, only intensifies the irony of Fielding's original praise. And her inability to sustain even the decision to guard her reputation, whatever the price, is simply proof of the extent to which she is subject to her passions.[23] Her lust for Joseph is, after all, no different from Slipslop's.

To her chambermaid's earlier decision, Fielding responds in much the same way. When, after the reconciliation, Slipslop offered to speak in Joseph's favor, but saw how adamant Lady Booby was against forgiving him, Fielding tells us that Slipslop "prudently dropped all such efforts" (I, ix), deciding that it would probably be best to forget about the handsome footman. Employing an ironic reversal of statement, Fielding then praises her decision:

[22] P. 328 (IV, xiii).
[23] Irwin Ehrenpreis makes a similar point in "Fielding's Use of Fiction: The Autonomy of *Joseph Andrews*", in *Twelve Original Essays on Great English Novels*, ed. Charles Shapiro (Detroit, 1960), p. 24.

... She at last gave up Joseph and his cause, and with a triumph over her passion highly commendable, walked off with her present, and with great tranquillity paid a visit to a stone-bottle, which is of sovereign use to a philosophical temper.[24]

The absurdity of this praise becomes clearest when we place Slipslop's "triumph" in its proper context. She overcomes her passion for Joseph with a series of rationalizations, each of which is more ridiculous than the one preceding, until she concludes that *any* male will be fair game for her lustful intent.

She considered there were more footmen in the house, and some as stout fellows, though not quite so handsome as Joseph; besides, the reader hath already seen her tender advances had not met with the encouragement she might have reasonably expected. She thought she had thrown away a great deal of sack and sweetmeats on an ungrateful rascal; and being a little inclined to the opinion of that female sect, who hold one lusty young fellow to be as good as another lusty young fellow, she at last gave up Joseph and his cause. . . .[25]

Fielding's praise of this decision is, therefore, part of his attempt to make the reader focus on the absurdity of Slipslop's rationalizing – a procedure which she must climax by having recourse to the stone-bottle; and this, when she is attempting to overcome a passion as strong as the sexual urge, is alone "of sovereign use". To insure that the reader will not mistake the irony, and to sustain the ironic pose to the end of the passage, Fielding concludes on the connotatively ironic notes of "tranquillity" (the result of the "prudent" reasoning) and "philosophical temper" (its cause).

In both instances, the ironic praise serves to emphasize the fact that Lady Booby and Slipslop come to the right conclusions for the wrong reasons. And like Slipslop, who proceeded from "reason" to the stone-bottle, Lady Booby drowns her passion and befuddles her mind in a paean to reason. The real (at least in the eyes of the world) gentlewoman and the aspirant to that title are very much sisters under the skin.

This satiric portrait of Lady Booby stands out most vividly when viewed against the background of Fielding's more general indict-

---

[24]   P. 29 (I, ix).
[25]   *Ibid.*

ment of the Boobys and their relationship to the inhabitants of the small village where the story begins and ends. In the description of little Joey's rise, it is immediately apparent that the ridicule is directed not at the hero of *Joseph Andrews* but at the Boobys and at the rural gentry in general (just as the irony of Fielding's introduction of Adams in I, iii is really directed at the bishop rather than at Adams). Fielding accomplishes this by the careful selection and placing of several connotatively ironic words in the short chapter (I, ii) which serves to introduce Joseph and to describe his meteoric rise from scarecrow to footman.

When little Joey proved unable to perform the "office" of scarecrow with any effectiveness, Sir Thomas transferred him from the fields to the kennels, where the young apprentice was to assist the huntsman in tending the nobleman's hunting dogs. Fielding tells us that Joey "was soon *transplanted* from the fields into the dog-kennel, where he was placed under the huntsman, and made what sportsmen term whipper-in". And when Joey proved to be as inept in the kennels as in the fields, "the poor boy . . . was . . . *transplanted* to the stable". Through the ironic connotations of this verb, Fielding suggests that Joey is little more than a vegetable or shallow-rooted shrub that can be moved at will from one corner to another of the Booby estate. The inhuman office of "keeping birds" is consonant with the inhuman connotations of "transplanted".

Yet Joey's star was on the ascendant, for after seven years, he finally rose to the rank of footman to the Lady Booby, thus progressing from keeping birds to dogs to horses to "keeping" a great lady, a progression that is later paralleled by the gradual formalizing of his name, for "Joey" becomes "Joseph" and, finally, "Mr. Joseph". Joey's great gift is his ability to charm each of these in turn, for the birds were as susceptible to his remarkably "great endowments" as was the great lady. To emphasize the absurdity of this final social "elevation", Fielding shifts to connotations of a different sort from those implied in "transplanted".

Joey was now *preferred* from the stable to attend on his lady, to go on her errands, stand behind her chair, wait at her tea table, and carry her prayer-book to church.[26]

[26] P. 5 (I, ii).

"Preferred" has the human connotations lacking in "transplanted", but they are now much too dignified. A nobleman may be "preferred" at court, but hardly a stable-boy at the Booby estate, his "great endowments" to the contrary. In the connotative progression from "transplanted" to "preferred" is thus epitomized on a mock scale the "social ladder" by which the larger world into which Joseph will venture is represented:

... It may not be unpleasant to survey the picture of dependence like a kind of ladder: as for instance; early in the morning arises the postilion, or some other boy, which great families, no more than great ships, are never without, and falls to brushing the clothes and cleaning the shoes of John the footman; who being drest himself, applies his hands to the same labours for Mr. Secondhand, the squire's gentleman; the gentleman in the like manner, a little later in the day, attends the squire; the squire is no sooner equipped than he attends the levée of my lord; which is no sooner over, than my lord himself attends the levée of the favourite, who, after the hour of homage is at an end, appears himself to pay homage to the levée of his sovereign. Nor is there, perhaps, in this whole ladder of dependence, any one step at a greater distance from the other than the first from the second; so that to a philosopher the question might only seem, whether you would choose to be a great man at six in the morning or at two in the afternoon.[27]

The absurdity of this purely chronological distinction between postilion and sovereign is then itself a mock analogue to the rise of a poor country boy of obscure origins from "autokropos" to scarecrow to footman.

Despite the ironic connotations of the words discussed above, Fielding never suggests that it is Joey who is pretentious or mean; his social aspirations are never the issue. The irony is really directed at those who manipulate Joey, Sir Thomas Booby and the class he represents in rural England. The connotations of "transplanted", for example, suggest a callousness toward humanity that was characteristic of many of the gentry. This attitude toward the poor parishioners of the Booby estate, implicit in the description of Joey, is made quite explicit on several subsequent occasions. In his introduction of Lady Booby, for example, Fielding tells us that

27   Pp. 147-8 (II, xiii).

my lady was a woman of gaiety, who had been blessed with a town education, and never spoke of any of her country neighbors by any other appelation than that of the Brutes.[28]

Lady Booby's subsequent behavior toward Mrs. Adams is consistent with this early characterization. In order to bring Didapper and Fanny together, Lady Booby suggests to her guests that they all visit the Adams family. The entire company (including Pamela!) embark upon this excursion as if they were going to observe animals in a zoo. And Lady Booby's only reaction to Mrs. Adams's awkward attempts at hospitality makes quite clear that to the noblewoman these people are indeed brutes, beasts, or animals.

The parson and his company retreated from the chimney side, where they had been seated, to give room to the lady and hers. Instead of returning any of the curtsies or extraordinary civility of Mrs. Adams, the Lady, turning to Mr. Booby, cried out, *"Quelle Bête! Quel Animal!"* [29]

Finally, one of Fielding's bitterest ironic attacks on the Boobys for their attitude toward the parish poor is contained in the description of the Lady's arrival from London. And once more these poor are described as if they were animals:

She entered the parish amidst the ringing of bells, and the acclamations of the poor, who were rejoiced to see their patroness returned after so long an absence, during which time all her rents had been drafted to London, without a shilling being spent among them, which tended not a little to their utter impoverishing; for, if the court would be severely missed in such a city as London, how much more must the absence of a person of great fortune be felt in a little country village, for whose inhabitants such a family finds a constant employment and supply; and with the offals of whose table the infirm, aged, and infant poor, are abundantly fed, with a generosity which hath scarce a visible effect on their benefactors' pockets? [30]

Since the Boobys were scarcely conscious of the existence – let alone the *difficulties* of existence – of their parishioners, it really makes little difference whether the latter are "Bêtes" or "Animaux" – or even vegetables. Just as looking at the poor offers pre-dinner

---

[28]   P. 8 (I, iii).
[29]   P. 312 (IV, ix).
[30]   P. 272 (IV, i).

diversion to the Boobys, so can the poor, as far as the Boobys are concerned, be fed with the "offals" of the knight's table and can, as with little Joey, be "transplanted" like shrubs. The highly suggestive connotations of this verb, therefore, epitomize some of the harshest social satire in *Joseph Andrews*.

The culmination of this condemnation of the Boobys and their society is Fielding's ironic characterization of their kinsman, Beau Didapper, the effeminate dandy who struts his pretentious way through the final book of *Joseph Andrews*. Not only does Didapper epitomize the physical and spiritual degeneracy of the nominal gentility, but through the "young gentleman" from London Fielding brings to an ironic conclusion the theme of prurient nakedness that began with Lady Booby in Book I, and resolves symbolically, if not literally, the social aspirations of Lady Booby's lustful chambermaid.

Fielding's description of Didapper stands in pointed contrast to the only other male who is described in such explicit detail, Joseph:

> Mr. Didapper, or beau Didapper, was a young gentleman of about four foot five inches in height. He wore his own hair, though the scarcity of it might have given him sufficient excuse for a periwig. His face was thin and pale; the shape of his body and legs none of the best, for he had very narrow shoulders, and no calf; and his gait might more properly be called hopping than walking.[31]

But with his description of Didapper's personality – a series of ironic poses in which Fielding combines understatement (litotes) with the undercut – Fielding makes more explicit the suggestion here that Didapper was sexually impotent.[32]

---

[31] P. 311 (IV, ix).

[32] Earlier attacks on the impotence of the beau confirm the deliberateness of Fielding's ironic focus here. See, for example, Fielding's description of the "fine young gentleman" in the Vision of Mercury and Charon at the River Styx in *The Champion* for May 24th. The ferryman refuses to allow anyone to enter the boat until he has first stripped himself of his clothing. "A fine young gentleman came next, he was mighty unwilling to strip, which we attributed to his affection for his clothes, which were a laced paduasoy; but, on his at last yielding to Mercury, we discovered another reason for his shyness" (*Works* [Henley], XV, p. 317). Cf. similar attacks in *Love in Several Masques* (*Works* [Henley], VIII, p. 21), *The Covent-Garden Tragedy* (*Works* [Henley], X, p. 116), the Epilogue to *The Univer-*

The qualifications of his mind were well adapted to his person. We shall handle them first negatively. He was not entirely ignorant; for he could talk a little French, and sing two or three Italian songs; he had lived too much in the world to be bashful, and too much at court to be proud: he seemed not much inclined to avarice; for he was profuse in his expenses: nor had he all the features of prodigality; for he never gave a shilling: no hater of women; for he always dangled after them; yet so little subject to lust, that he had, among those who knew him best, the character of great moderation in his pleasures. No drinker of wine, nor so addicted to passion, but that a hot word or two from an adversary made him immediately cool.[33]

The real comedy of Didapper's role in *Joseph Andrews* rests in large part on our recognizing that whenever he appears, it is to play the part of an ineffectual lover. When we first see him, he is attacking Fanny, who is easily able to repulse him, "as our spark was not of the Herculean race" (IV, vii). Didapper has the unique distinction of being the only man in *Joseph Andrews* whom Fanny is able to repulse successfully. Unable to persist, Didapper leaves behind a servant to pander for him. On his second appearance, he renews his pusillanimous attempts on Fanny, this time by offering "a rudeness to her with his hands". When Joseph boxes his ear, Didapper draws his sword on the unarmed assemblage. But Fielding again undercuts this one "manly" action: after Mr. Booby assures the beau that he will have satisfaction (which Didapper never pursues), Fielding tells us that "the beau now sheathed his hanger, and taking out a pocket-glass, and vowing vengeance all the time, readjusted his hair" (IV, xi). On his third appearance as a "lover", the naked Didapper attempts to rape Fanny, only to discover the naked Slipslop – who, preferring with "wonderful presence of mind" to use this occasion to restore the reputation of her "impregnable chastity", decides to repulse him. Thus Didapper is rejected not only by the most desirable female in *Joseph Andrews*, but by the least desirable. Didapper is nothing more than what Fielding originally called him, a "dangler" after women, not a lover, for he cannot succeed by any means, good looks, charm, rhetoric, subterfuge, a pander, or sheer force. Consequently, all that is left for him is the empty, pitiful boast of an amour that never took place, for, as Fielding tells us, on the morning after the night-walking episode in Booby Hall,

Lady Booby produced the diamond button [discovered in Slipslop's bedroom], which the beau most readily owned, and alleged that he was very subject to walk in his sleep. Indeed, he was far from being ashamed of his amour, and rather endeavoured to insinuate that more than was really true had passed between him and the fair Slipslop.[34]

Fielding's irony here forces the reader to concentrate on the sharp antithesis between the connotations of "amour" on the one hand, and the repulsiveness of the "lovers" – as well as their respective motives – on the other. Didapper's intention was the rape of the person he thought was Fanny; Slipslop's was the seduction of the person she thought was Joseph. Furthermore, we know that Didapper's insinuation that "more than was really true had passed between him and the fair Slipslop" was mere talk – and ridiculous talk at that, for who but a gaudy, spindly-legged London beau (the frequent object of Fielding's contempt throughout his early writings) [35] would boast of having made love to Slipslop, and then

---

[34]   P. 337 (IV, xv).

[35]   Didapper is one of the several foolish beaus in Fielding's works who boast of "amours" that never occurred. Master Owen Apshinken in *The Grub-Street Opera*, for example, is a less polished Didapper, but he shows the same traits as his more famous descendant. When Margery rejects him, Owen resolves to "go back to Molly and make sure of her, if possible – or I may be in danger of dying half a maid yet; for the devil take me, if I ha'n't a shrewd suspicion that, in all my amours, I never yet thoroughly knew what a fine woman was. I fancy it often happens so among us fine gentlemen.

Air LVIII.
The idle beau of pleasure
        Oft boasts a false amour,
As breaking cit his treasure,
        Most gaudy, when most poor;
But the rich miser hides the stores he does amass,
And the true lover still conceals his happy lass."

(*Works* [Henley], IX, p. 270).

In *The Universal Gallant* Mondish describes beaus in the following manner: "These sort of gentlemen are the only persons who engage with women without danger. The reputation of an amour is what they propose, and what they generally affect: for, as they indulge their vanity at the

spoken of her as fair? This is Fielding's final condemnation of the foolish, empty, impotent beau.

Didapper's mistaken "leap" into Slipslop's bed also sets the stage for what proves to be Fielding's final comment on prurient nakedness masquerading as endangered innocence, for in our view of the naked Slipslop clinging fast to the naked Didapper "and roaring out, 'O thou villain! who has attacked my chastity, and, I believe, ruined me in my sleep; I will swear a rape against thee, I will prosecute thee with the utmost vengeance' " we are treated to the *reductio ad absurdum* of that earlier scene where her mistress, also "innocently" naked in bed, says to Didapper's astounded counterpart: "I have trusted myself with a man alone, naked in bed; suppose you should have any wicked intentions upon my honour, how should I defend myself?"

From another point of view, however, Didapper's false boast of an "amour" – which, significantly, Slipslop makes no attempt to refute – represents for her an ironic triumph rather than an ignoble gesture of self-exposure, for the "reputation of an amour" with one who is regarded as a gentleman by the world to which she aspires – even though it is only the same Didapper whom she had repulsed the night before – brings her as close as she will ever come to her intriguing mistress. This wholly imaginary "amour" has, for the moment at least, made Slipslop a gentleman's "gentlewoman". Fielding never mentions her again.

Finally, in Didapper's masquerade as Joseph as he leaps into what he thinks is Fanny's bed, hero and mock hero are symbolically joined, making more explicit what previously had been only vaguely suggested. Fielding's ironic insistence upon Didapper's gentility and sexual potency has – as with Slipslop and Lady Booby – an added function in the novel inasmuch as what Fielding ironically attributes to Didapper are in reality the virtues of the hero of

---

price of all that is dear to a woman, the world is good natur'd enough to make one person ridiculously happy, at the expense of making another seriously miserable" (*Works* [Henley], XI, p. 91). Cf. also Captain Spark's comments (pp. 112-114, 135), Mrs. Bellamant's remarks about Gaywit in *The Modern Husband* (*Works* [Henley], X, p. 35), and the more general attack on the beau in the "Essay on Conversation", *Works* (Henley), XIV, p. 265.

Joseph Andrews, the ironically transformed Priapus. Although Didapper is ostensibly a gentleman, it is Joseph – and not the beau – who has the qualities an 18th-century reader would ordinarily associate with the term – and who by the end of the novel actually becomes a gentleman in name, in dress, as well as in deed. And Didapper's boast of an "amour" that could not have taken place stands in ironic juxtaposition to Joseph's refusal of three frankly solicited invitations to bed and to his eventual marriage to the most desirable female in the book.

If Beau Didapper symbolizes the moral and particularly the physical degeneracy of part of the upper stratum of English society – and Fielding was certainly not unique among neoclassical satirists in viewing the beau or the "fine gentleman" in this light – Betty, the chambermaid at the Tow-wouse's inn, is to Fielding, conversely and perhaps paradoxically, symbolic of the health that can be found in the humble servants' quarters of an English country inn, for Betty acts according to the dictates of her "good nature", a prime virtue to Fielding,[36] rather than by calculation. Unlike Lady Booby, who assumes the false pose of rationality to conceal an honest passion, Betty has not a modicum of affectation about her. Accordingly, although she is subjected to a certain amount of ridicule, her character is not undermined, for whatever her faults, she remains a "good-natured wench". And the irony Fielding employs to help characterize her makes this immediately apparent. In this respect alone, the portrait of Betty is quite distinct from those I have been discussing.

Fielding's chief technique with Betty is again connotative irony, but unlike his characterizations of Slipslop, Lady Booby, and Beau Didapper, the terms of irony never involve moral judgments of any kind. Instead the exaggerated praise of the connotations becomes a vehicle for what borders on the mock heroic. Betty is given qualities which are only absurd because of their incongruity – qualities which amuse us rather than arouse our moral indignation – for she is garbed consecutively in those connotations more appropriate to the convent, classical rhetoric, and the militant heroine of epic

---

[36]   Battestin, pp. 64-76.

tradition. For example, after recovering from the unfortunate consequences of an affair with an ensign of foot, Betty resolved, Fielding tells us, to resist the temptations of sexual indulgence and that she "seemed to have vowed a state of perpetual chastity" (I, xviii). Now, "vowed" (as synonymous with "resolved") is indeed denotatively relevant here, but its connotations in a context that contains references to "nunneries", "good-nature, generosity, and compassion", (in the opening paragraph of the chapter devoted to Betty's history), and, finally, to "a state of perpetual chastity" serve only to emphasize the comic incongruity between Betty and the very concept of chastity – perpetual or not.

We are, of course, never in suspense over Betty's capacity for maintaining her nun-like "vow". And Fielding's confirmation of our expectations provides another example of connotative irony employing complimentary connotations.

She was long deaf to all the sufferings of her lovers, till one day, at a neighbouring fair, the rhetoric of John the hostler, with a new straw hat and a pint of wine, made a second conquest over her.[37]

Insofar as rhetoric is basically the art of persuasion, John the hostler is a rhetorician; John is persuasive and Betty is persuaded. But how appropriate are the connotations of "rhetoric" to John? To 18th-century readers, "rhetoric" would normally connote formal oratory, learning, the liberal arts (of which rhetoric was a part) – indeed, a broad spectrum of literary expression. To Johnson, it was "the act of speaking not merely with Propriety, but with Art and Elegance". And according to an earlier definition, rhetoric was the "Arte of speaking Finely".[38] Applied to an 18th-century hostler at a roadside inn in the particular circumstances in which John found himself with Betty, these connotations can be only absurd.[39] That John was effectively persuasive is suggested by the fact that he causes Betty to strip herself of her moral resolutions

---

[37] P. 72 (I, xviii).
[38] Dudley Fenner, *The Arte of Rhetorike* (London, 1588), p. 1 (cited in Bullitt, p. 81).
[39] That it was not uncommon for writers to use "rhetoric" in an ironic sense is indicated by the OED's reference to its "ironical and jocular use" in the 18th century.

– as well as of her clothes – again, both a figurative and literal nakedness. But the ultimate irony of "rhetoric" lies in our awareness that John probably did not really need the skills of a rhetorician to overcome Betty since, in addition to the enticements of a new straw hat and a pint of wine, her constitution was by nature composed, as Fielding says earlier, "of those warm ingredients, which, though the purity of courts or nunneries might have happily controlled them, were by no means able to endure the ticklish situation of a chambermaid at an inn" (I, xviii).

Later, in his description of Mr. Tow-wouse's seduction of Betty, Fielding uses a term that is as connotatively revealing as *rhetoric*. When Betty is ejected from Joseph's room, it suddenly occurs to her that she has forgotten to make her master's bed (considering her emotional state, it is not surprising that she would think "accidentally" of beds). When she enters his room, Mr. Tow-wouse sees an opportunity to fulfill what has obviously been a long-suppressed desire:

As soon as she saw him, she attempted to retire: but he called her back, and, taking her by the hand, squeezed her so tenderly, at the same time whispering so many soft things into her ears, and then pressed her so closely with his kisses, that the *vanquished* fair one, whose passions were already raised, and which were not so whimsically capricious that one man only could lay them, though, perhaps she would have rather preferred that one; the *vanquished* fair one quietly submitted, I say, to her master's will, who had just attained the accomplishment of his bliss, when Mrs. Tow-wouse unexpectedly entered the room. . . .[40]

Vanquished has obvious denotative validity in this context, but the connotations of the word are ridiculous: after all, even "raped" seems inappropriate here, let alone "conquered". Considering Betty's sexually promiscuous nature in general and her present state of arousal in particular, "vanquished" tends to give Betty credit for far more restraint than she has – or ever will have. The "vanquished fair one" has, in fact, agreed "quietly" rather than been forced to submit to her master's will.

[40]   P. 73 (I, xviii).

The irony directed at Betty, it should be emphasized, focuses almost exclusively on the absurdity of her sexual lapses, but never in such a manner as to suggest that Fielding condoned promiscuity, for he genuinely did value chastity as a moral virtue.[41] The irony here simply supports the comedy inherent in what is really a stock situation, and Betty is no more capable of chastity than was Pamela of promiscuity. It is the comedy of the fat gourmet resolutely determined to resist the fat roast duckling placed on the board before him. What we know of the human condition makes us able to predict with virtual certainty what will inevitably happen. Accordingly, there is little – if any – corrosive satire here. Betty is neither a hypocrite nor devious in any respect; she is simply a weak vessel.

With many of the other characters in *Joseph Andrews*, verbal irony functions in much the same way that it does in the satiric portraits described above, although on a more modest scale. To some of the minor people, in fact, it provides the only comic dimension they possess and slightly rounds them, to use Forster's phrase. Consider, for example, the brief characterization of the constable in Book I who allows the highwayman to escape. Fielding's description of the escape is really an extended ironic defense of the constable's integrity. Fielding introduces him with what appears to be fairly obvious denotative irony, for he attributes to the constable wisdom, caution, and sagacity, and the skill of a chess-player who is guilty of nothing more than an understandable oversight.

But human life . . . very much resembles a game at chess; for as in the latter, while a gamester is too attentive to secure himself very strongly on one side of the board, he is apt to leave an unguarded opening on the other; so doth it often happen in life; and so did it happen on this occasion; for whilst the cautious constable with such wonderful sagacity had possessed himself of the door, he most unhappily forgot the window.

The thief who played on the other side, no sooner perceived this opening, than he began to move that way; and finding the passage easy, he took with him the young fellow's hat, and without any ceremony stepped into the street and made the best of his way.[42]

[41]   Battestin, pp. 114-118.
[42]   P. 57 (I, xvi).

But Fielding's handling of the allegations made against the constable's integrity and the inverted syllogism with which he climaxes his defense severely modify our initial impression of the constable.

> The constable hath not been discharged of suspicion on this account; it hath been said, that not being concerned in the taking of the thief, he could not have been entitled to any part of the reward, if he had been convicted; that the thief had several guineas in his pocket; that it was very unlikely he should have been guilty of such an oversight; that his pretence for leaving the room was absurd; that it was his constant maxim, that a wise man never refused money on any conditions; that at every election he always had sold his vote to both parties, &c.
>
> But notwithstanding these and many other such allegations, I am sufficiently convinced of his innocence; having been positively assured of it, by those who received their informations from his own mouth; which, in the opinion of some moderns, is the best and indeed only evidence.[43]

The constable's wisdom, caution, and sagacity are really connotatively, rather than denotatively, ironic, for, given the circumstantial evidence, and the "opinion of some moderns", the constable was far more shrewd ("prudent" in Slipslop's sense) than ignorant or incautious. It is left to Mrs. Tow-wouse to underscore the irony of Fielding's defense by providing us with the one bit of information that would have given the entire scene away had it been presented earlier – the fact that the constable's name was Tom Suckbribe.

But where, one may ask, are Joseph and Parson Adams in this discussion of verbal irony in *Joseph Andrews*? There are several reasons for their absence. For one thing, Joseph and Adams – and even Fanny – are painted with much broader strokes than those I have discussed. To be sure, they are subjected to a certain amount of good-humored ridicule, but through other than primarily verbal techniques. With Adams, as we shall see later, one of the major characterizing devices is dramatic irony, although there are occasions when Fielding does employ some of the verbal forms, particularly understatement. And aside from the introduction to I, iv, verbal irony is seldom used to suggest traits of character in Joseph or, for that matter, in Fanny. In Joseph's case, Fielding relies more

---

[43]   Pp. 57-8 (I, xvi).

upon a series of dramatic juxtapositions, allusions to things external
to the novel (Priapus, the biblical Joseph, Oedipus), and parody
rather than upon subtle nuances of character.

Another reason for Fielding's relatively modest use of verbal
irony in characterizing Joseph and Adams is the inappropriateness
of the technique, for verbal irony is perhaps the most harshly corrosive of the satiric devices; its primary aim is to undermine character by constantly discrediting what seems on the surface to be
creditable, and, ultimately, to reflect the fundamental hypocrisy
and affectation of those people on whom such irony is lavished.
Beneath it all, they are as untrustworthy as the poses they assume.
In an important sense, then, verbal irony strongly underscores the
Pelagian basis of Fielding's morality [44] by constantly warning us in
Joseph Andrews of the dangers of placing too much faith in nominal distinctions or in man's professions of goodness, for actions, he
feels, are ultimately the only true index of character and good
works the only means to salvation. Fielding does, after all, make a
better case for the morality of the sexually promiscuous Betty than
for that of the always prudent and sexually continent Slipslop, or
for that of the maritally faithful Mrs. Tow-wouse, who "was as true
to her husband as the dial to the sun" (I, xviii). Thus, although he
constantly reminds us of Adams' inconsistencies – one of the glories
of the book – Fielding never attempts to undermine either his
character or Joseph's.

The most compelling reason, however, for the particular focus
of Fielding's verbal irony in *Joseph Andrews* is the presence of a
much larger double irony – to use Mr. Empson's phrase – that
creates so much of the tone and texture of this novel. This double
irony exists in the proximity of the novel's surface to its own potential parody. The effect is somewhat similar to that in Restoration heroic plays which are peculiarly satisfying to us, as Mr. Empson has observed, only because they come so close to parodying
themselves [45] – yet, at their best, never quite do. Such parody is, of
course, potential in any highly stylized work or highly mannered
situation, whether it be Restoration drama, classical ballet, the

[44] Battestin, see chapter II.
[45] Empson, *Some Versions of Pastoral*, p. 55.

Hollywood western, or in such staples of comedy as the pursuit of the innocent virgin (from the farm) by the corrupt villain (from the city), or the emotional meeting of two long-separated lovers. Whether we recognize it or not, this potential for parody or self-ridicule is always present and ready to be tapped by the satirist. In this respect, *Shamela* is less of a shock when we realize that it was beneath the surface of *Pamela* all along.

In *Joseph Andrews*, there are innumerable situations in which such parody is potentially present even if *Pamela* had never been written. These are the situations in which verbal irony is almost always present, for it is through verbal irony that the parodic vein is most obviously tapped. The seduction scenes in Book I, of course, come most immediately to mind, for they are the most obviously mannered scenes in *Joseph Andrews* – so much so, in fact, that in his first letter to Pamela, Joseph compares Lady Booby's actions to those he had seen in stage-plays in Covent-Garden (I, vi). A less obvious but perhaps more compelling example of such parodic encroachment is the emotional meeting of Joseph and Fanny in II, xii, a scene that has been taken as seriously illustrative of Fielding's essential benevolence.[46] However, to take this scene seriously in any sense is to miss the presence of the parody and of the subtle ironic jab at the end of the scene that enables us to see how close to the surface parody really is. The narrator's self-conscious comment on his own description of Joseph and Fanny embracing is, of course, an obvious indication of just how closely this highly-mannered scene totters on the brink of absurdity.

But, O reader! when this nightingale, who was no other than Joseph himself, saw his beloved Fanny in the situation we have described her, canst thou conceive the agitations of his mind? If thou canst not, wave that meditation to behold his happiness, when, clasping her in his arms, he found life and blood returning into her cheeks; when he saw her open her beloved eyes, and heard her with the softest accent whisper, "Are you Joseph Andrews?" – "Art thou my Fanny?" he answered eagerly; and pulling her to his heart, he imprinted numberless kisses on her lips, without considering who were present.

[46]   For example, see Battestin, p. 110.

If prudes are offended at the lusciousness of this picture, they may take their eyes off from it, and survey parson Adams dancing about the room in a rapture of joy.[47]

But what is less obvious is the degree to which Joseph's song and Fielding's description of Adams' Aeschylus "expiring" on the fire function as parodic comment on themselves as well as upon the sentimental scene which they circumscribe. Joseph's song is highly stylized, employing all of the conventions of the risqué pastoral love song of Restoration comedy – but so obviously and excessively as to make us immediately suspect that Fielding may have pushed it beyond its legitimate limits. The final stanza is worth quoting for what follows:

> Advances like these made me bold.
>   I whisper'd her, – Love, we're alone. –
> The rest let immortals unfold:
>   No language can tell but their own.
> Ah, Chloe, expiring, I cried,
>   How long I thy cruelty bore!
> Ah, Strephon, she blushingly replied,
>   You ne'er was so pressing before.[48]

What brings out the full significance of the song – particularly this final stanza – and of its relationship to the meeting of the lovers is Fielding's connotatively ironic reference to another "expiration" in this scene, that of Adams' beloved Aeschylus, who also lay smoldering, not in the heat of passion, but in the literal fire of a roadside ale house.

... As soon as the first tumults of Adams' rapture were over, he cast his eyes towards the fire, where Aeschylus lay expiring; and immediately rescued the poor remains, to wit, the sheepskin covering, of his dear friend, which was the work of his own hands, and had been his inseparable companion for upwards of thirty years.[49]

The connotative irony of "expiring" here serves two functions: By offering an immediate and absurd contrast to Strephon's sexual "expiring", it pushes Joseph's song to the point where the parody

[47] P. 145 (II, xii).
[48] P. 144 (II, xii).
[49] P. 145 (II, xii).

now blatantly protrudes rather than suggests itself. But even more significantly, the connotatively ironic expiration of poor Aeschylus – a "dear friend", an "inseparable companion" – and the unambiguous sexual "expiring" of Strephon together point to a third "expiration" which encompasses the elements of both, for it is Fanny who "expires" at almost the moment Strephon does and falls "backwards in her chair", *apparently* devoid – as we are told later – of both "life and blood". It is this third – and the only false – expiration that thus brings the parody already implicit in the sentimental "union" of the long-separated lovers closest to the surface. For our present purposes, however, it is important to recognize that it is verbal irony that accomplishes what a direct comic device could never do here: it just barely touches upon this undercurrent of parody that is always beneath such highly artificial situations, but only enough to intimate its presence, for to bring it completely to the surface would be to reduce its comic effectiveness.

In this respect, verbal irony extends well beyond its use as a method of satiric characterization. Although this tapping of the parodic vein has the effect of ridiculing the characters involved, it does not by itself undermine the fundamental virtue of those who are, to use Fielding's own phrase, "good-natured". An awareness of this dual function of verbal irony would thus explain Fielding's treatment of Adams, Joseph, and Fanny. The parodic undercurrent that is implicit in many of the scenes in which they appear defines the degree to which Fielding treats them as comic characters and, at times, ridicules them. But such ridicule seldom, if ever, involves undermining their characters through verbal irony. They are, after all, neither more nor less absurd than they appear to be. What saves them ultimately, however, is the spontaneity of their natures – a spontaneity, incidentally, that the harshly satirized characters do not possess, because their behavior is too studied, too calculated. However ridiculous Joseph may appear as he defends his chastity before Lady Booby by mouthing the moralistic platitudes that he had learned from parson Adams, what saves him is his spontaneous admission that "I am glad [Lady Booby] turned me out of the chamber as she did; for I had once forgotten every word parson Adams had ever said to me" (I, x). It is at points like this in the novel that parody disappears, for it is impossible "to turn a good act to ridicule".

The symbolic manifestation of this spontaneity is, as I have suggested earlier in this chapter, the nakedness of the innocent, just as the nakedness of the corrupt is associated with actions that are deliberate, calculated, and formalized. It is verbal irony that first brings this thematic pattern into focus and strongly supports it throughout *Joseph Andrews*, from the first comparison of Adams to a newborn "infant just entered into the [world]" (I, iii) to Fanny's disrobing on her wedding night (IV, xvi). This nakedness is, in every instance, either literal or figurative or both. There are innumerable examples of symbolic nakedness in *Joseph Andrews*, but perhaps a few illustrations may indicate the relationship of verbal irony to this important structural pattern.

A short time after Lady Booby's attempt on Joseph's vaunted chastity, an attempt which, as I have already noted, is characterized by Fielding's covering her artful and corrupt nakedness with the cloak of false innocence, Joseph also appears naked, but here as a result of ill fortune (actually someone else's corruption) rather than his own artifice, for he has been stripped and robbed by a pair of highwaymen. Significantly, it is the postilion, the one charitable human being on the coach, who makes the explicit connection between Joseph's nakedness and true innocence, for he compares Joseph to a newborn babe, "as naked as ever he was born" (I, xii). Like the newborn babe, not only is Joseph innocent, but his nakedness has made him virtually helpless in a world in which few people are inclined by nature to relieve human distress. Indeed, it is the reaction of Joseph's world to the innocent man in distress – as represented by the naked Joseph – that Fielding concentrates on in the remainder of this chapter and for most of the remainder of Book I.

Aside from the reference to "the spotless example of the amiable Pamela", there is no irony directed at Joseph in this scene. Instead, Fielding directs his irony at the passengers in the coach – particularly at the "ingenious" gentleman who makes the "wonderfully facetious ... allusions to Adam and Eve" and "who said many excellent things on figs and fig-leaves", and at the lawyer, who does not "[depart] from his profession". But for the most part, Fielding simply lets the passengers speak for themselves, which exposes them perhaps even more effectively than the verbal irony. Fielding's intention in this scene should by now be apparent, for the behavior of the passengers serves, in effect, to strip them as naked spiritually as Joseph had been physically. In contrast to the charitable postilion, however, who achieves moral stature by his voluntarily stripping himself (literally) of his great-coat, the passengers expose themselves as hollow men whose moral natures shrivel up the more they talk, for there is ugliness and moral deformity beneath their clothing. It is the lawyer's "several very pretty jests" that neatly sum up the scene, for in his obscene remarks, nakedness once more degenerates to the prurience of the earlier seduction scenes.

Verbal irony also strongly supports the nakedness theme as it manifests itself in the many references to dressing and undressing in *Joseph Andrews*. For example, it is the good-natured Betty's action in providing the naked Joseph with a bed in the inn and a shirt from her hostler sweetheart that prompts the ill-natured and half-naked Mrs. Tow-wouse to "sally out in quest of the unfortunate Betty", with "half her garments on, the other half under her arm" (I, xii). And it is this same charitable hostler who, as we later (in I, xviii) discover, is a "rhetorician", skillful enough to cause Betty to strip herself of her moral resolutions – as well as of her clothes.

These references to nakedness culminate in the dressing – and undressing – of both Joseph and Fanny in Book IV. With Joseph, the irony is directed once more at those who assume the title of "gentleman" – like Beau Didapper – in contrast to those who are by their good nature truly genteel. Joseph is attired in a suit of Mr. Booby's, a suit which, significantly, does not fit the squire:

Joseph was soon dressed in the plainest dress he could find, which was a blue coat and breeches, with a gold edging, and a gold waistcoat with the same: and as this suit, which was rather too large for the squire, exactly fitted him, so he became it so well, and looked so genteel, that no person would have doubted its being well adapted to his quality as his shape; nor have suspected, as one might, when my

Lord –, or Sir –, or Mr. – appear in lace or embroidery, that the tailor's man wore those clothes home on his back which he should have carried under his arm.[50]

These satiric allusions to noblemen and gentlemen are reinforced by an ironic undercut in the following chapter, where Joseph acquires a new title to go along with the new clothing, for he is now to be known as "Mr. Joseph, he having as good a title to that appelation as many others; I mean that incontested one of good clothes" (IV, vi).

In Joseph's case, the nakedness theme reaches its climax in his baring his breast to reveal the strawberry mark – a literal nakedness that once again has symbolic value, for in Joseph's final – and voluntary – nakedness is symbolized the triumph of genuine innocence. It is the undressing of Joseph that becomes the real triumph and not the attiring of Joseph in clothing which can only be borrowed and never his own. In Joseph's innocence is thus epitomized his real virtue, a virtue that needs neither the nominal elegance of a title nor the sartorial elegance of fine apparel to define it.

With Fanny, this theme manifests itself primarily in two important scenes near the end of the novel. In the earlier of the two, Fanny stands partially naked before Joseph, who has just rescued her from Didapper's servant. Once again, it is the self-parody lurking potentially beneath the highly stylized surface that is hinted at by the verbal irony.

Fanny now begged Joseph to return with her to parson Adams, and to promise that he would leave her no more. These were propositions so agreeable to Joseph, that, had he heard them, he would have given an immediate assent; but indeed his eyes were now his only sense; for you may remember, reader, that the ravisher had torn her handkerchief from Fanny's neck, by which he had discovered such a sight, that Joseph had declared, all the statues he ever beheld were so much inferior to it in beauty, that it was more capable of converting a man into a statue, than of being imitated by the greatest master of that art. This modest creature, whom no warmth in summer could ever induce to expose her charms to the wanton sun, a modesty to which perhaps they owed their inconceivable whiteness, had stood many minutes bare-necked in the presence of Joseph, before her apprehen-

[50] P. 288 (IV, v).

sion of his danger, and the horror of seeing his blood, would suffer her once to reflect on what concerned herself; till at last, when the cause of her concern had vanished, an admiration at his silence, together with observing the fixed position of his eyes, produced an idea in that lovely maid, which brought more blood into her face than had flowed from Joseph's nostrils. The snowy hue of her bosom was likewise changed to vermilion, at the instant when she clapped her handkerchief around her neck. Joseph saw the uneasiness she suffered, and immediately removed his eyes from an object, in surveying which he had felt the greatest delight which the organs of sight were capable of conveying to his soul; – so great was his fear of offending her, and so truly did his passion for her deserve the noble name of love.[51]

But even more significant is the description of Fanny's undressing on her wedding night, for in this scene is the culmination of the nakedness-innocence theme. Whereas with the passengers in the coach, with Slipslop, Didapper, and Lady Booby, their literal and figurative undressing reveals only moral and sometimes even physical deformity, with Fanny, as with Joseph earlier, "undressing . . . was more properly discovering, not putting off ornaments".

She was soon undressed; for she had no jewels to deposit in their caskets, nor fine laces to fold with the nicest exactness. Undressing to her was properly discovering, not putting off ornaments; for as all her charms were the gifts of nature, she could divest herself of none. – How, reader, shall I give thee an adequate idea of this lovely young creature! The bloom of roses and lilies might a little illustrate her complexion, or their smell her sweetness; but to comprehend her entirely, conceive youth, health, bloom, neatness, and innocence, in her bridal bed; conceive all these in their utmost perfection, and you may place the charming Fanny's picture before your eyes.[52]

And when Joseph joins her in bed, Fielding slyly closes the scene by contrasting them once more to the spiritually impoverished – if nominally and sartorially elegant – nobility.

Joseph no sooner heard she was in bed, than he fled with the utmost eagerness to her. A minute carried him into her arms, where we shall leave this happy couple to enjoy the private rewards of their con-

---

[51]   Pp. 303-4 (IV, vii).
[52]   Pp. 345-6 (IV, xvi).

stancy; rewards so great and sweet, that I apprehend Joseph neither envied the noblest duke, nor Fanny the finest duchess that night.[53]

There is no verbal irony in this scene, but even without it, it is not difficult to perceive the parodic potential implicit in the very tone of Fielding's description. However, by constantly causing us to focus on the frequent shifts and reversals through which the naked-ness-innocence theme has progressed throughout the novel, verbal irony has brought us up to this thematic resolution. This basically structural function of verbal irony thus joins the satiric and parodic as the only means by which some of the comic depths of *Joseph Andrews* can be plumbed.

[53]   P. 346 (IV, xvi).

V

DRAMATIC IRONY

Dramatic irony is one of those unfortunate misnomers that has become firmly entrenched in modern criticism, for the type of irony it denotes is no more properly the province of the drama than it is of the novel or the periodical essay, or – for that matter – of the lyric poem. But it is quite distinct from rhetorical irony, which, as I have already noted, was, for all practical purposes, the only type of irony the 18th century was conscious of using.

Whereas rhetorical irony depends upon the ambiguity of a statement made directly to a reader by the ironist, dramatic irony depends exclusively upon the ambiguity inherent in what a character (fictitious or otherwise) says or does. Dramatic irony is truly dramatic, then, only in the conventional absence of authorial intrusion. Its ambiguity usually involves a contrast between degrees of awareness of character and spectator or reader, a contrast which is specifically defined by "the sense of contradiction felt by the spectators of a drama who see a character acting in ignorance of his condition".[1]

In Fielding's early works, dramatic irony manifests itself through several techniques, all of which are traditional to dramatic irony as it was employed in comic works of the 18th century and earlier. These range from the relatively obvious verbal ambiguity of double-edged language to the more subtle ambiguities of character and relationship. With double-edged language, Fielding simply plays upon the contrast between what a character says and what

---

[1] Sedgewick, *Of Irony*, p. 49. See also David Worcester, *The Art of Satire* (Cambridge, Mass., 1940), pp. 111-121; and Alan R. Thompson, *The Dry Mock: A Study of Irony in Drama* (Berkeley, 1948), pp. 29-47.

the omniscient spectator knows through the context to be true. In its simplest form, this device functions primarily as a means of dramatic emphasis or dramatic anticipation. In one of Fielding's early farces, *The Letter-Writers; or a New Way to Keep a Wife at Home*, double-edged language is the chief dramatic ironic technique which he employs to support the comedy of a stock situation. Two foolish old men, Mr. Softly and Mr. Wisdom, concoct a scheme to keep their young wives at home and thus minimize the ever-present risk of cuckoldry. Each writes an anonymous letter to the other's wife, "threatening to murder her in her chair the first time she goes abroad, unless she lays twenty guineas under a stone".[2]

The scheme works as expected for Mr. Wisdom, but not for Mr. Softly. Mrs. Softly, to show that she is not afraid, goes abroad even more than before, but heavily guarded and armed – at great additional cost to her distressed husband. Each of the old men, nevertheless, is firmly convinced that his wife remains faithful to him: Wisdom because his wife is always at home now, Softly because his wife goes abroad only "in the best company". What the spectator knows is that each wife is managing easily to deceive her husband – and with the same lover, Rakel, a dissolute young army officer. To further complicate this situation, neither wife knows that she is sharing Rakel with the other. Mr. Softly, however, in spite of the apparent success of the plot, is beginning to have qualms about its expense.

Mr. Softly. I am sure I have severely paid for all the terrors I have given my wife: if I could bring her to be only as bad as she was before I should think myself entirely happy. In short, brother, I have found by woeful experience, that mending our wives is like mending our constitutions, when often after all our pains we would be glad to return to our former state.

Mr. Wisdom. Well, brother, if it be so, I have no reason to repent having been a valetudinarian. – But let me tell you, brother, you do not know how to govern a wife.

Mr. Soft. And let me tell you, brother, you do not know what it is to have a woman of spirit to govern.

Mr. Wisd. A fig for her spirit, I know what it is to have a virtuous

[2]   *Works* (Henley), IX, p. 182.

wife; and perhaps I am the only man in town that knows what it is to keep a wife at home.

Mr. Soft. Brother, do not upbraid me with my wife's going abroad: if she doth, it is in the best company. And for virtue – for that, Sir, my wife's name is Lucretia – Lucretia the second; and I don't question but she's as chaste as the first was.

Mr. Wisd. Ay, ay, and I believe so too – But don't let the squeamishness of your conscience put a stop to my success: and let me tell you, if you are not advantaged by the strategem, you will be disadvantaged by the discovery, for if you put such a secret into your wife's bosom, let me tell you, you are not Solomon the second.[3]

Here, in the praise each husband gives to his wife's chastity – as well as in Mr. Softly's wish that he could bring his wife "to be only as bad as she was before" – is simple verbal ambiguity, or double-edged language. The irony lies in the certainty of their protestations: the more positive they are of their wives' chastity, the farther they are from the truth, and the greater the irony.

The importance of Fielding's use of dramatic irony at this point in *The Letter-Writers* becomes apparent when we note that this scene precedes the revelation of the bitter truth to both old men. Letters from their wives to Rakel are found in his pockets when he is discovered hiding beneath a table in Mrs. Wisdom's room. These are read by Sneaksby, the clerk, at Rakel's arraignment the morning after his capture.

Sneaks. [*Reads*] "Be here at the time you mention, my husband is luckily out of the way. I wish your happiness be, as you say, entirely in the power of

"ELIZABETH WISDOM."

Mr. Wisd. What's that? Who's that?

Sneaks. Elizabeth Wisdom.

Mr. Wisd. [*Snatches the letter.*] By all the plagues of hell, my wife's own hand too.

Mr. Soft. I always thought she would be discover'd, one time or other, to be no better than she should be. [*Aside.*]

Mr. Wisd. I am confounded, amazed, speechless.

Mr. Soft. What's the matter, brother Wisdom? Sure your wife doth not hold correspondence with these people; your wife! that durst not go abroad for fear of them; who is the only wife that her husband can keep at home!

---

[3]   *Ibid.,* IX, p. 197.

Mr. Wisd. Blood and furies, I shall become the jest of the town.

Sneaks. May it please your worship, here is one letter more, in a woman's hand too.

Mr. Soft. The same woman's hand, I warrant you.

Sneaks. [*Reads.*] "Sir, your late behaviour hath determined me never to see you more: if you get entrance into this house for the future, it will not be by my consent; for I desire you would henceforth imagine there never was any acquaintance between you and

"LUCRETIA SOFTLY."

Mr. Wisd. Ha!

Mr. Soft. Lucretia Softly! – Give me the letter – Brother Wisdom, this is some counterfeit.

Mr. Wisd. It must be so. Sure it cannot come from Lucretia the second; she that is as chaste as the first Lucretia was – She correspond with such as these, who never goes out of doors but to the best company in town!

Mr. Soft. 'Tis impossible![4]

The double-edged language of the first scene, therefore, illustrates the simplest functions of dramatic irony: it emphasizes the foolishness of these two old men, and their inability to see what is going on beneath their very noses; and it foreshadows the exposure that is to follow. Their fall from the heights of blissful ignorance is much greater to the omniscient spectator once it has been prepared for by such inordinate boasting.

A more complex form of dramatic irony as verbal ambiguity is Fielding's use of double-edged language both for its own sake as well as to suggest a conflicting relationship of which the characters – never the spectators – are totally ignorant. In *The Letter-Writers*, the irony of the scenes discussed above stems entirely from what Mr. Softly and Mr. Wisdom say. Although the spectator is aware that these two foolish old men are not what they think they are, the roles they play with respect to one another are at no time in conflict. In another of Fielding's plays, on the other hand, *Rape Upon Rape, or The Justice Caught in His Own Trap*, we are presented with a series of characters who not only speak with double-edged language but also oppose one another in a variety of ways. It is this added element of conflict that serves to intensify the

[4]   *Ibid.*, IX, pp. 199-200.

original ambiguous speech and to amplify significantly the spectator's awareness of dramatic irony.

In *Rape Upon Rape*, Ramble has attempted to ravish the virtuous Hilaret, who he thinks is a street-walker. Hilaret's cries for help are heard by the watch, who rescue her and convey both before Squeezum, the dishonest magistrate. Ramble is sent to the constable's house to await arraignment, and it is there that he meets his old friend, Constant, who was arrested during a street fight in which he was attempting to aid another young lady who was being accosted by a ruffian. Unknown to Ramble, Constant is Hilaret's lover and was on his way to elope with her. At the constable's house, Sotmore, Ramble's perpetually inebriated friend, is berating Ramble for having fallen into his predicament:

Sot. . . . Did I not tell thee, thou wert strolling off to some little dirty whore! and you see the truth of my prophecy.

Ramb. Thou art in the right: it was not only a whore, but the most impudent of all whores − a modest whore.

Const. A modest whore! let her be married to an honest attorney, by all means.

Ramb. And sent together to people his majesty's plantations.

Sot. Modesty, now-a-days, as often covers impudence as it doth ugliness. It is as uncertain a sign of virtue as quality is, or as fine clothes are of quality.

Ramb. Yet to do her right: the persuasions of the justice could not prevail with her to perjure herself.

Sot. Conscientious strumpet! She hopes to pick your pocket another time, which it were charity to thee to wish she might: for, if thou escapest this, she certainly will have an opportunity. . . . It it not enough to make a man rail, to have parted with a friend happy in the night, and to find him the next morning in so fair a way to − Death and damnation! shew me the whore; I'll be revenged on her and the whole sex. If thou art to be hanged for ravishing her, I'll be hanged for murdering her. Describe the little mischief to me. Is she tall, short, black, brown, fair? In what form hath the devil disguised himself?

Ramb. In a very beautiful one, I assure you: she hath the finest shape that ever was beheld, genteel to a miracle; then the brightest eyes that ever glanced on a lover, the prettiest little mouth, and lips as red as a cherry; and for her breasts, not snow, marble, lilies, alabaster, ivory, can come up to their whiteness; but their little, pretty, firm, round form, no art can imitate, no thought conceive −

Oh! Sotmore, I could die ten thousand millions of times upon them –
   Scot. You are only likely to die once for them.
   Const. All these raptures about a common whore, Ramble? [5]

This incisive irony of Constant's two remarks lends to this passage
a dramatic effectiveness that is immediately apparent; but this is
the result of more than mere verbal ambiguity. The spectator is
suddenly aware that beneath the friendship of Constant and
Ramble lies reason enough for the bitterest enmity, for would-be
ravisher and lover share a common relationship to Hilaret; but,
obviously, neither is aware at the time of this relationship.

   In the next scene, the dramatic irony is heightened by the fact
that the spectator's knowledge is now shared by all except Constant, for Hilaret has arrived to search for him. Refusing to believe
the charges against her lover, particularly since they have been
brought by Squeezum, Hilaret rushes into Constant's arms – to the
amazement of Ramble, who soon senses the truth. Hilaret then
discovers the reason for Constant's arrest.

Hil. And was you in that scuffle that parted me and my maid in
Leicester Fields?
   Const. It was there this unfortunate accident happened, while I was
going to the place of our appointment.
   Hil. It had like to have occasioned another to me, which, that I
escaped, I am to thank this gentleman.
   Ramb. Oh, Madam! your most obedient, humble servant. Was it
you, dear madam?
   Const. Ha! is it possible my friend can have so far indebted me! –
This is a favour I can never return.
   Ramb. You over-rate it, upon my soul you do; I am sufficiently
repaid by this embrace.
   Const. I can never repay thee. – Wouldst thou have given me
worlds, it could not have equalled the least favour conferred on this
lady.
   Ramb. I should have conferred some favours on her indeed, if she
would have accepted them. [*Aside.*]
   Hil. I am glad it is to Mr. Constant's friend I am obliged.
   Sot. Yes, you are damnably obliged to him for his character of
you. [*Aside.*]

---

[5]   *Ibid.*, IX, pp. 115-117.

Const. My dear Hilaret, shall I beg to hear it all? I can have no pleasure equal to finding new obligations to this gentleman.

But before Hilaret can respond, Ramble interrupts with a story he has concocted on the spur of the moment and which supports the misconception Constant already has of the encounter between his sweetheart and friend. When Ramble describes Hilaret's attacker as "a very rude fellow", Hilaret decides to go along with the story, but she cannot resist making Ramble squirm in discomfort a bit longer.

Hil. The most impudent fellow, sure, that ever was born!
Ramb. A very impudent fellow, and yet a very cowardly one; for the moment I came up he quitted his hold, and was gone out of sight in the twinkling of an eye.
Const. My dear Ramble, what hast thou done for me!
Ramb. No obligation, dear Constant! I would have done the same for any man breathing. . . .

Ramble then concludes his account and Constant is overcome with gratitude:

Const. Oh, my friend! May Heaven send me an opportunity of serving thee in the same manner! [6]

In this scene, the double-edged language suggests a new aspect of the conflicting relationship, for in the reiteration of Constant's desire to return the "favour", the spectator becomes aware of would-be ravisher and lover inadvertently drawing even closer together. The irony here, however, is intensified by Constant's ignorance, which keeps both the spectator and the other characters in a constant state of suspense – an effect Fielding is careful to preserve by having Ramble say to himself, with a discomfort that only the spectator and Hilaret, if she overhears the remark, can easily sense: "May that be the only prayer which it denies to Constant." [7] The final irony of this comedy is provided by the fact that Constant has already unwittingly returned this favor by rescuing that unknown lady whom he was later accused of attempting to rape and who in reality is Ramble's supposedly drowned wife.

[6]   *Ibid.*, IX, pp. 118-119.
[7]   *Ibid.*, IX, p. 119.

A more subtle form of the ironic relationship described above depends wholly on situational rather than verbal ambiguities. The spectator cannot rely upon double-edged language to lead him to the irony; he must be able to perceive it through the positions the characters take with respect to one another – between what the characters *think* their relationship to be and what the omniscient spectator *knows* it to be. The first part of *Pasquin* illustrates Fielding's ability to sustain at length this type of dramatic irony. In the rehearsal of the comedy, "The Election", Fielding employs this technique as a means of gradually exposing the relationship that exists between Trapwit and the personages of his own play. Trapwit thinks of his play quite simply as "an exact representation of nature", and gives no indication that his characters are guilty of any kind of impropriety. He sees bribery as a purely comic, almost farcical, affair that one accepts as lightly as the marriage of Colonel Promise and Miss Mayoress. To the actor who performs the role of Lord Place, he advises:

Trap. You, Mr. that act my Lord, bribe a little more openly, if you please, or the audience will lose that joke, and it is one of the strongest in my whole play.
Lord Place. Sir, I cannot possibly do it better at the table.
Trap. Than get all up, and come forward to the front of the stage. Now you gentlemen that act the Mayor and Aldermen, range your-selves in a line; and you, my Lord, and the Colonel, come to one end and bribe away with right and left.
Fustian. Is this wit, Mr. Trapwit?
Trap. Yes, sir, it is wit; and such wit as will run all over the king-dom.[8]

The dishonesty that besmirches the whole electoral process is little more than what Trapwit calls a "joke" at which spectators may chuckle in bland amusement.

Consistent with Trapwit's inability to see the true nature of his "joke" is his subordinating the election scenes to what he insists is the main plot, the courtship and marriage of Colonel Promise and Miss Mayoress. Aside from being a satiric thrust at the practices of contemporary comic dramatists, this misconception of the plot

[8] *Ibid.*, **XI**, p. 173.

of "The Election" emphasizes Trapwit's inability to understand the significance of his own play. The corruption of the characters – with the sole exception of one apparently honest alderman whom Trapwit, significantly, calls "a fool" who was created only "to set off the rest" – is a comic prelude to the swiftly consummated intrigue of two very minor people. What looms largest in the play is, through an ironic reversal, least important in Trapwit's mind. And what is to Trapwit simply an objective representation of society is, more properly, its vicious condemnation. Beneath the veneer of innocent comedy (the "joke") is a core of cynical satire, a fact obvious to all except the "author". What emerges from this first part of *Pasquin*, therefore, is the picture of a bustling dramatist whose sole function is to create a series of scenes that will amuse his audience. He sees the stage as nothing more than a vehicle for light entertainment, even when the material he employs suggests knavery and immorality at its blatant worst.

The effect of presenting the rehearsal within this dramatic ironic framework is to intensify the several other ironic situations in the play, because the spectator is always conscious that these situations are constantly projected to him through what is, in effect, a distorted lens. The first conversation between Lord Place, Mrs. Mayoress, and her daughter illustrates the manner in which Fielding keeps the spectator aware of this irony-within-irony. In this conversation, Lord Place attempts to persuade Mrs. Mayoress to pander for her daughter, the fairly obvious irony resulting from the ladies' naiveté and Lord Place's simple transference of the terms of moral behavior to that of immoral.

Lord Place. I cannot but with pleasure observe, madam, the polite taste Miss shows in her choice of entertainments; I dare swear she will be much admired in the *beau monde*, and I don't question but will be soon taken into keeping by some man of quality.
Miss. Keeping, my Lord!
Lord Place. Aye, that surprise looks well enough in one so young, that does not know the world; but, Miss, every one now keeps, and is kept; there are no such things as marriages now-a-days, unless merely Smithfield contracts, and that for the support of families; but then the husband and wife both take into keeping within a fortnight.
Mrs. Mayoress. My Lord, I would have my girl act like other young

ladies; but she does not know any men of quality; who shall introduce her to 'em?

Lord Place. That, Madam, must be your part; you must take a house, and see company; in a little while you may keep an assembly, and play at cards as high as you can; and almost all the money that is won must be put into the box, which you must call, *paying for the cards*; though it is indeed paying for your candles, your clothes, your lodgings, and in short everything you have. I know some persons who make a very considerable figure in town, whose whole estate lies in their card-box.

Mrs. May. And I have been so long contented to be the wife of a poor country tradesman, when I might have had all this happiness![9]

The climax to the irony of this scene occurs when Lord Place leaves the room and Mrs. Mayoress, in persuading her daughter to prostitute herself, employs a syllogistic argument that is as perverse as it is irrefutable:

Mrs. May. He is a prodigious fine gentleman.
Miss. But must I go into keeping, Mama?
Mrs. May. Child, you must do what's in fashion.
Miss. But I have heard that's a naughty thing.
Mrs. May. That can't be, if your betters do it; people are punished for doing naughty things; but people of quality are never punished; therefore they never do any naughty things.[10]

As harshly ironic as this scene might appear by itself, its ultimate effect stems from the degree to which the spectator is made conscious of the obtuseness of the playwright who created it. As the scene begins, Trapwit is telling Fustian of the source of his inspiration:

Sir, in this play, I keep exactly up to nature; nor is there anything said in this scene that I have not heard come out of the mouths of the finest people of the age. Sir, this scene cost me ten shillings in chair-hire, to keep the best company as it is called.[11]

The irony of the conversation between Lord Place and the two silly women is thus intensified significantly by the ironic frame that has been created by the situational ambiguity, for the scene is presented

---

[9]   *Ibid.*, XI, pp. 179-80.
[10] *Ibid.*, XI, p. 181.
[11] *Ibid.*, XI, p. 179.

to us by a man who sees in it only a perfect imitation of nature. That such a perversion of moral behavior may indeed be true to life makes it more rather than less ironic.

The ironic frame functions in the same manner elsewhere in the first part of *Pasquin*, where Fielding's purpose is to attack illogic, hypocrisy, crass self-interest, and immorality, by showing Trapwit's characters pretending to possess the contrary virtues. Within the limits of the play-within-the-play, Fielding places these characters in a series of ambiguous situations where the spectator can perceive the dramatic tension between, on the one hand, what the characters think they are and what he can see them to be in reality, and, on the other, what Trapwit conceives them to be.

An extension of this ironic relationship through situational ambiguity involves Fielding's use of a conflict of valid but contradictory roles played by the same character, a conflict that becomes, in effect, a form of dramatic self-betrayal, as in his exposure of Pamela in *Joseph Andrews*. In attempting to defend Fanny's character against the combined onslaught of Lady Booby, Squire Booby, and Pamela, Joseph says to his sister:

– "Sure sister, you are not in earnest; I am sure she is your equal, at least." – "She was my equal," answered Pamela; "but I am no longer Pamela Andrews, I am now this gentleman's lady, and, as such, am above her. – I hope I shall never behave with an unbecoming pride; but, at the same time, I shall always endeavour to know myself, and question not the assistance of grace to that purpose." [12]

We are confronted here with the ironic juxtaposition, on the one hand, of Richardson's virtuous heroine, and Fielding's ignoble social snob, and, on the other, of her insistence that "I shall always endeavour to know myself" as opposed to our awareness that self-knowledge (in any sense other than that of social rank) is a virtue to which this Pamela could never possibly aspire.

The most sustained use of this second type of situational ambiguity occurs in Fielding's description of Parson Adams in politics. The disclosure of Adams' political career (II, viii) modifies his apparently irreproachable honesty as neatly as the news of the

[12]   P. 300 (IV, vii).

drowning of little Dick overturns his stoicism. By showing the reader the honest curate acting, with naive relish, the role of the dishonest political entrepreneur, Fielding underlines with dramatic emphasis that delightful streak of inconsistency that has made Parson Adams at once both ridiculous and lovable. The irony stems from the reader's awareness of Adams playing simultaneously two contradictory roles, and this ultimately constitutes a form of self-betrayal.

While waiting for Joseph and the coach to catch up with him, Adams meets a hunter whose professed patriotism and willingness to talk prompt the Parson to relate the lengthy story of his early adventures into English politics. Adams tells how his political power was derived from a nephew who had risen to the position of alderman of a municipal corporation. Because of this nephew, the Parson's interest was constantly solicited by candidates for office. Flattered and pleased by this attention, Adams never once considered his situation objectively. He saw nothing wrong with taking advantage of his nephew's obligations to him.

He was a good lad, and was under my care when a boy; and I believe would do what I bade him to his dying day. Indeed, it looks like extreme vanity in me, to affect being a man of such consequence as to have so great an interest in an alderman; but others have thought so too. . . .[13]

As a result, Adams was a potent force in local politics: indeed, without exception, every candidate he influenced his nephew to support was elected.

When the rector attempted to bribe him to influence the alderman's vote in favor of Colonel Courtly, Adams indignantly informed the rector that voting was a matter of individual conscience and that he "would by no means endeavour to influence . . . [the alderman] to give it otherwise" (II, viii). But when the rector accused him of lying and indicated that it was known that Adams had already interfered in favor of Esquire Fickle, the Parson retorted with what comes remarkably close to the politician's callous insistance that the end justifies the means. He did influence his

---

[13]   P. 121 (II, viii).

nephew's vote, Adams admitted, but it was really to save the
church. ". . . It was at a season when the church was in danger,
and when all good men expected they knew not what would happen to us all" (II, viii). The climax of his defense is his indignant
refusal to retract his promise to Fickle. "I then answered boldly,
If he thought I had given my promise, he affronted me in pro-
posing any breach of it" (II, viii). Unaware of the inconsistency of
his position, Adams has presented an ethical justification for an
unethical act.

The Parson's relationship with Sir Oliver Hearty involved him
in the more serious problem of bribery. When Colonel Courtly,
now campaigning against Sir Oliver, offered to make Adams chap-
lain of his regiment in return for the alderman's support, Adams
refused, and turned instead to Sir Oliver, "who told us he would
sacrifice everything to his country". Sir Oliver had little difficulty
winning the election. When it became obvious that Sir Oliver was
as viciously disreputable as Fickle and showed more interest in
hunting than in government, Adams displayed a surprising lack of
concern for such blatant disregard of obligation and – even more
astonishing – praised the "worth" of Sir Oliver!

However he was a worthy man, and the best friend I ever had; for,
by his interest with a bishop, he got me replaced into my curacy, and
gave me eight pounds out of his own pocket to buy me a gown and
cassock, and furnish my house. He had our interest while he lived,
which was not many years.[14]

From the brief sketch Fielding has given of Sir Oliver, it seems
improbable that his generosity to Adams resulted from pure
benevolence. The favor and gift were payment for a political obligation incurred during the election. Obviously, Adams does not see
this as a bribe, probably because Sir Oliver's gifts were tendered
more discreetly than Colonel Courtly's outright offer. Sir Oliver's
character did not, apparently, taint the gifts – first of a patronage
position, then of money – for Adams shows no uneasiness about
having accepted them.

When Sir Oliver died, Adams had another opportunity to

[14]   Pp. 122-3 (II, viii).

demonstrate his political power, "for all the world knew the interest I had with my good nephew, who was now a leading man in the corporation" (II, viii). This time Adams cast his support in favor of Sir Thomas Booby because it "did me good to hear him discourse on affairs, which, for my part, I knew nothing of" (II, viii). Obviously, Sir Thomas had no difficulty winning the election. There is not even mention made of his opponent. This election is of particular significance for the insight it affords into the growth of Adams' political power. During the first campaign, Adams and his nephew evidently had to work hard to get Fickle elected. "I persevered, and so did my nephew, in the esquire's interest, who was chose chiefly through his means" (II, viii). But by the time Adams came to support Sir Thomas Booby, he was experienced in the ways of elections and his nephew had risen in the corporation. He no longer had to "persevere". His description of the Booby election is a classic of brevity and self-confidence: "I engaged my nephew in his interest, and he was elected" (I, viii).

The death of his nephew saw the decline – but not the demise – of Adams' political aspirations.

Since my nephew's death, the corporation is in other hands; and I am not a man of that consequence I was formerly. I have now no longer any talents to lay out in the service of my country.[15]

Adams then makes his most significant statement, epitomizing with unintentional irony the creed of the political entrepreneur: ". . . To whom nothing is given, of him can nothing be required" (II, viii).

The allusion here to the parable of the talents (*Matthew* XXV: 14-30) is worth particular notice because it is the closest Fielding comes in this chapter to indicating the contradictory roles played by Adams. Through the implied comparison, Fielding makes him at once both the now profitless servant and the harsh master who passes final judgment. The repetition of the allusion at the conclusion of the chapter not only substantiates the importance of the parallel but climaxes the irony of the parson's self-betrayal. Adams is talking about the possibility of ordination for his thirty-year old son:

[15]   P. 123 (II, viii).

"... He is a good boy; and if Providence should throw it in his way to be of as much consequence in a public light as his father once was, I can answer for him he will use his talents as honestly as I have done." [16]

There is no reason to doubt Adams' sincerity at the chapter's end, even though the concluding sentence is heavily ironic to the reader who is fully aware of the discrepancies in the parson's behavior. Whenever Adams strayed over the line between political honesty and dishonesty, it was not a conscious act. When he lied to the rector about influencing the alderman, Adams knew and admitted his equivocation; but he was not aware of his subsequent and more serious inconsistencies. And when he accepted the gifts from Sir Oliver, it probably never occurred to him that they were political booty. His final claim, then, was made in all sincerity; it was simply not true.

It would be more accurate to blame the parson's misfortunes on his folly in becoming involved at all in politics as much as on the specific things he did, for politics in the mid-18th century was an area where the distinctions were more often between different kinds of dishonesty than between simple honesty and dishonesty. When faced with a choice between candidates such as Fickle and Colonel Courtly, Sir Oliver Hearty and Colonel Courtly, and Sir Thomas Booby and his unnamed opponent, 18th-century voters had little hope for good government. A factor of more specific relevance to Adams' political career, however, and one which demonstrates more clearly Fielding's motives in thus exposing Adams, was the frequent charge that the clergy constituted too powerful a force in local politics. Regardless of which side they chose, the country parsons were customarily regarded as mighty men at election time. Henry Fox even complained that the clergy, together with the attorneys, were sufficient to "carry any election". [17]

More serious than the general interference of the clergy was the matter of bribery. Many clerics could be bought at election time –

---

[16]   P. 124 (II, viii).
[17]   Keith G. Feiling, *The Second Tory Party, 1714-1832* (London, 1951), p. 11.

a fact that was common knowledge to the horde of dishonest men who constantly sought political office for personal aggrandizement. Walpole, among others, was acutely aware of the power of the clergy – as well as of their weaknesses. In preparation for the general elections of 1708, for example, he took particular care to win over the Norfolk clergy, particularly the country parsons.[18] And in *Pasquin*, Fielding ironically treats clerical bribery as a commonplace in 18th-century elections. Mrs. Mayoress, attempting to convince her husband to vote for Lord Place and Colonel Promise, points out to him that "a place is no bribe – ask the parson of the parish if a place is a bribe".[19] And in the following scene, Fielding strikes again at clerical "pliability":

> *3rd Voter.* An't please your honour, I have read in a book called Fog's Journal, that your honour's men are to be made of wax; now, Sir, I have served my time to a waxwork maker, and desire to make your honour's regiment.
> *Colonel Promise.* Sir, you may depend on me.
> *3rd Voter.* Are your officers to be made of wax too, Sir? because I would prepare a finer sort for them.
> *Col.* No, none but the chaplain.
> *3rd Voter.* O! I have a most delicate piece of black wax for him.[20]

The intent of the ironic self-betrayal in this chapter is not to suggest a specific parallel between Adams and these corrupt clergy, but it is to indict Adams for allowing himself to be caught up in and innocently support the corruption and dishonesty that so frequently besmirched 18th-century politics. Martin Battestin, however, is quite correct in pointing out that Fielding did not intend Adams to be an object of contempt – as Barnabas and Trulliber were [21] – for aside from his vanity, Adams does display those characteristics of the true priest as Fielding had defined them in *The*

---

[18]   Plumb, p. 137.

[19]   *Works* (Henley), XI, p. 183.

[20]   *Ibid.*, XI, pp. 184-5. See also *The Champion* for April 19, 1740. For a contrasting view of what Fielding thought the clergy should be, see *The Champion* for April 12, 1740 and Dr. Harrison's reasons for refusing a bribe from a nobleman in return for his "interest" in helping elect the nobleman's candidate (*Amelia*, XI, ii).

[21]   Battestin, Chapter 7.

Champion for April 19, 1740.[22] Even in his ironic introduction of the parson at the beginning of *Joseph Andrews* (I, iii), Fielding's point is not to attack Adams but the bishop who rewards a fifty-year old clergyman who has a wife and six children with "a handsome income of twenty-three pounds a year" – and this in spite of such qualities as had actually "endeared and well recommended him to [the] bishop". The picture of Adams that thus emerges from this story of his political career is not that of a hypocrite but of a man whose naiveté, refusal to profit from experience, and indefatigable faith in the power of virtue prevent him from perceiving the consistency with which he himself betrays his cherished ideals.

These techniques of dramatic irony in Fielding's early works were as conventional as his plays. Double-edged language was, as I have already pointed out, a traditional ironic device long before the mid-18th century and was still popular at the time Fielding began his literary career as a playwright in 1728. In fact, Gay's *Beggar's Opera*, which made its first appearance that same year, was probably an important influence on Fielding's use of double-edged language in the ironic songs that he inserted into several of the plays – songs which, as in the *Beggar's Opera*, were sung to popular tunes of the day. Compare, for example, Signior Opera's song (Air VIII) to the Goddess of Nonsense in *The Author's Farce* to Air XLIV in the *Beggar's Opera*, sung by Macheath to his gang. Both songs were sung to the same tune, "Lillibullero":

> [Signior Opera]
> Let the foolish philosopher strive in his cell,
>   By wisdom, or virtue, to merit true praise;
> The soldier in hardship and danger still dwell,
>   That honour and glory may crown his last days;
>   The Patriot sweat,
>   To be thought great;
> Or beauty all day at the looking-glass toil;
>   That popular voices
>   May ring their applauses,
> While a breath is the only reward of their coil.

[22] *Works* (Henley), XV, p. 283.

But would you a wise man to action incite,
  Be riches proposed the reward of his pain:
In riches is centered all human delight;
  No joy is on earth but what gold can obtain.
    If women, wine,
    Or grandeur fine,
Be most your delight, all these riches can;
  Would you have men to flatter?
  To be rich is the matter;
When you cry he is rich, you cry a great man.[23]

             [Macheath]
The modes of the court so common are grown
  That a true friend can hardly be met;
Friendship for interest is but a loan,
  Which they let out for what they can get.
    'Tis true, you find
    Some friends so kind,
Who will give you good counsel themselves to defend.
    In sorrowful ditty,
    They promise, they pity,
But shift you, for money, from friend to friend.[24]

Both songs are cynical reductions of conventional moral values: merit is reduced to riches, virtue to avarice, moral stature to affluence.

Fielding's other dramatic ironic techniques, if not as intrinsic to dramatic irony as double-edged language, were at least common to many of the restoration and 18th-century dramas that Fielding so admired and imitated in his early plays. But in general, Fielding was never able to achieve with dramatic irony what Gay, for example, did in the *Beggar's Opera*, or Congreve in *The Way of the World*. As effective as his dramatic irony was in the plays, it never really becomes much more than a complementary device; it never succeeds in creating tone or mood, as Gay's irony does so clearly in the *Beggar's Opera*. Where Fielding does approach the achievement of a Gay or a Congreve is in *Joseph Andrews*, but here the dramatic irony is strongly supported by a heavy overlay of rhetori-

23 *Ibid.*, VIII, pp. 239-40.
24 *Eighteenth-Century Plays*, ed. Ricardo Quintana (New York, 1952), p. 222.

cal irony. More important, perhaps, than the presence of other ironies is Fielding's greater originality and maturity as a novelist; the imitativeness of the plays was, in general, too inhibiting upon manner as well as substance. But perhaps the ultimate weakness of the dramatic irony in the plays stems from Fielding's discomfort in having to efface himself as a dramatist. His irony was much more effective when he could intrude consciously into his work and establish with his reader a relationship that was constantly being modified by the ambiguities of rhetorical irony.

VI

CONCLUSION

When we approach Fielding as a playwright, a periodical essayist, or a novelist – rather than as an ironist exclusively – a new set of considerations is immediately suggested. For example, how do specific techniques affect particular works or genres? Is there any chronological development from work to work either within the techniques themselves or in the kinds and frequency of techniques that appear? What might such a development indicate about Fielding's use of irony in the specific works involved? Or, finally, since the two novels of this period are the only works which afford the opportunity for a genuine comparative examination, what techniques does Fielding seem to favor in *Joseph Andrews* and *Jonathan Wild*, and how might a comparison of the techniques in each illuminate some of the basic differences in the irony of these two works? The following offers some brief answers to some of these questions.

In the plays, Fielding employs dramatic irony most frequently as a satiric device. Occasionally it is the chief vehicle for the satire, but more often it simply complements what has already been shaped into satire by other means. Dramatic irony is most prominent in the satiric plays written near the beginning of Fielding's playwriting career – between March 1730 (*The Author's Farce*) and August 1731 (*The Grub-Street Opera*) – and at the end – between April 1736 (*Pasquin*) and May 1737 (*The Historical Register*). Aside from *Rape Upon Rape* (a satirical comedy) and *The Letter-Writers* (a farce), all of the plays written during these periods are burlesques.[1] In the non-satiric plays written during the initial and interim years (between February 1728 and February 1730 and between January 1732 and February 1735), dramatic irony is relatively insignificant.

The mask, as noted earlier, is central to the satire of *Tom Thumb*, but does not appear elsewhere in the plays. It is, after all, a literary rather than a dramatic technique. Significantly, Fielding's first *persona* is as satirically effective and as skillfully delineated as any that appear later in *The Champion*. On the other hand, the verbal techniques that Fielding employs in the non-dramatic satiric prefaces and dedications are relatively unsophisticated: denotative irony appears most frequently, but only as blame-by-praise with antithetical denotations, the simplest and most common of Fielding's verbal techniques. Reversal of statement is the only other verbal technique of any importance in the plays. On occasion, Fielding employs both of these as irony by implication.

Fielding's attack on Dr. John Misaubin in the burlesque dedication to *The Mock Doctor*, an adaptation of Moliere's *Le Médecin malgré lui*, is a good illustration of this relative lack of sophistication of the verbal irony in the plays. The irony is simple to perceive, the meaning always transparent. Employing only the denotative technique noted above, Fielding merely praises Misaubin for qualities which most 18th-century readers would immediately recognize to be false. No attempt is made to develop with any subtlety the ironic attack on the boorish quack who achieved such notoriety with his "little pill".[2] In general, the same can be said about the verbal irony in the other ironic prefaces and dedications, particularly those in which Fielding attacks Walpole (*The Historical Register*)[3] and Rich (*Tumble-Down Dick*, or *Phaeton in the Suds*).

[1] I have accepted Leo Hughes' suggestion that Fielding's plays might be most conveniently classified as either comedies of manners, farces, satirical comedies, or burlesques. See Leo Hughes, "The Influence of Fielding's Milieu Upon his Humor", *Studies in English, The University of Texas*, XXIV (1944), pp. 269-297.

[2] Cross, I, pp. 131-2.

[3] It is possible that the dedication to Walpole of *The Modern Husband* was also intended to be ironic, but there is no proof of this. This may be another example of irony so subtle as to be wasted.

In *The Champion*, a dominant technique is, as I have pointed out earlier, the ironic mask. The reason for this is fairly obvious: the form of the *Champion* essays, all of which Fielding pretended were written by hands other than his own, is particularly well suited to the use of the *persona*, offering as it does a convenient method by which the spokesman can characterize himself. Unlike his practice in the plays and the novels, in *The Champion* Fielding wants to focus attention on the speaker as much as on the substance of the essay. There is, however, no significant development in Fielding's use of the ironic mask from *Tom Thumb* through *The Champion*. Scriblerus Secundus is as carefully conceived as any of the *personae* that follow and certainly more effective as a satiric device than some of the later masks in *The Champion*.

In those *Champion* essays where he disguises himself behind a simple ironic pose rather than behind a full-blown mask, Fielding employs almost all of the verbal techniques described earlier, the single exception being connotative irony, which appears not at all. Of these, Fielding relies on denotative irony most frequently. Although his intention in most of the heavily ironic essays is to carry on his earlier dramatic attacks on corruption in politics, literature, and popular taste, as well as on characteristic foibles of human nature, the relative sophistication of the verbal irony tends to give many of these essays a comic quality that mitigates to a great extent much of the harshness of the satire. Even among those written by *personae*, there are none of the prognostications of gloom and despair over an impending collapse of the cultural world that were characteristic of the writings of many of the Tory satirists of the early 18th century.[4] On the other hand, the verbal irony is concentrated enough to create in the satiric essays of *The Champion* a style quite distinct from that of the *Tatler* and *Spectator*. Fielding's early periodical satires may be comic in tone and manner, but they ultimately lack the lightness and grace of Addison's and particularly Steele's.

Fielding employs dramatic irony in *Joseph Andrews* as situa-

---

[4]   See Louis Bredvold, "The Gloom of the Tory Satirists", in *Eighteenth Century English Literature*, ed. James L. Clifford (New York, 1959), pp. 3-20.

tional ambiguity, which here, unlike his practice in the plays, he uses primarily for characterization. On the other hand, he does not develop the narrator in *Joseph Andrews* into a *persona*. The narrator is never more than Henry Fielding assuming a series of ironic poses, none of which is ever fully delineated. There are several reasons for this. For one thing, it is clear that the presence of a *persona* would only have detracted from the centrality in the novel of the comic characterizations, the narrative development, and even the parody of *Pamela*. Of considerably more importance in Fielding's decision to employ this kind of narrator was his imitation of Marivaux's self-conscious narrators in *La Vie de Marianne* (1731-41) and *Pharsamon, ou les folies romanesques* (1737). As Wayne Booth has shown,[5] Marivaux's novels were a major influence on Fielding's narrative method. In *Pharsamon* in particular can be found almost every one of the techniques of narrative intrusion that Fielding uses in *Joseph Andrews*.[6]

Fielding's earlier uses of the intrusive narrator-author device also tend to justify his practice here in *Joseph Andrews*. In the plays, for example, Fielding is quite sensitive to the relationship of the author to his own work. In *Pasquin*, as I have already shown, Trapwit is unaware of the implications of his own play. This is intended to be ironic, and Trapwit is as much the butt of Fielding's ridicule as the characters Trapwit himself presents. On the other hand, Medley in *The Historical Register* is the perfect antithesis to Trapwit, for he is fully aware of the implications of his own work, and thus illustrates a different kind of satiric function in his play. The tension that is established in the relationship of author (narrator) to work to reader thus becomes an important aspect of Fielding's satiric design. Fielding as the self-conscious narrator in *Joseph Andrews* can also, then, be regarded as an extension of Medley, for he is not simply fully aware of the implications – satiric and otherwise – of his own created work, but he even manipulates his reader by adopting constantly shifting and deliberately ambiguous poses.

---

[5] Wayne Booth, "The Self-conscious Narrator in Comic Fiction Before *Tristram Shandy*", *PMLA*, LXVII (1952), pp. 163-85.
[6] *Ibid.*, p. 171.

This manipulation of the reader – ironic both in manner as well as intention – serves a purpose that is clearly beyond the scope of the *persona's* function, for it is as much specifically satiric as it is traditionally comic. Such satiric manipulation, however, involves only a certain type of reader of *Joseph Andrews* – the sentimentalist who allows himself to become so emotionally entangled with the narrative that he fails to see that he is as much the butt of Fielding's ridicule as the fictional characters themselves. Thus when Fielding stops the action in III, x in order to "divert" the reader with an apparently irrelevant dialogue between the poet and the player, he is doing more than merely imitating Marivaux's elaborate delaying tactics; [7] his verbal irony is, in effect, a means of engaging in a cat and mouse game with the sentimental reader who would take seriously the battle of the chamberpot and the dirty mop and the peculiar array of combatants: a trouserless parson, a resolute male virgin, a pandering captain, and a trembling but chaste milkmaid.

This ridicule of the sentimental reader, however, was not just another attack of a neoclassical satirist on the uncultivated, amorphous "mob", but a quite specific lashing out at the admirers and adulators of Richardson's *Pamela*. The extent to which those readers hung breathless upon every turn of events is, of course, an old story. Aaron Hill's family and friends are said to have been so moved by some of Hill's readings of *Pamela* that they often left the room to weep privately; and at Slough, the villagers are said to have rung the church bells when their reader came to Pamela's marriage.[8] Fielding's reaction to Richardson's novel was certainly not simply an objection to the supposedly shoddy morality of the book but to the enthusiasm with which it was accepted as well. The reader who thus looked for the same thing in *Joseph Andrews* that he found in *Pamela* might discover, in the final analysis, that he himself was the object of an ironist's ridicule. If *Shamela*, then, constituted a direct attack upon Richardson's novel, *Joseph Andrews* may have been, in this respect at least, an attack on

[7] *Ibid.*, p. 174.
[8] F. Homes Dudden, *Henry Fielding, His Life, Works and Times* (Oxford, 1952), I, p. 313.

Richardson's readers, an aim that could not have been achieved if
Fielding had developed his disguise beyond the most transparent
of ironic poses.

The major ironic technique in *Joseph Andrews* is, as I have already noted, verbal irony. Fielding employs in the novel all of the
techniques and their variations described in Chapter III, and leans
rather heavily on the various types of connotative and denotative
irony, understatement, and the undercut. One of the remarkable
things about the verbal irony of *Joseph Andrews*, however, is the
fact that it is dominated by connotative irony – a technique that
appears here for the first time in Fielding's writings. This is undoubtedly a reflection of its value in characterization which, in
Joseph Andrews, is the chief use to which Fielding applies most of
the verbal techniques.

In *Jonathan Wild*, two denotative techniques (blame-by-praise,
employing antithetical denotations, and praise-by-blame) and one
connotative (with complimentary connotations) dominate the irony.
Of these three, Fielding uses the first most often. He makes little
use of the remainder of the techniques, several appearing not at all
in *Jonathan Wild*. Dramatic irony appears occasionally and only as
situational ambiguity. Again, the techniques are used primarily to
characterize. As in *Joseph Andrews*, the narrator in this novel
is not a *persona* but Henry Fielding merely assuming an ironic
pose – one which, it must be added, he does not maintain consistently.[9]

In general, Fielding's progression from the drama to the periodical
essay to the novel limited the extent of the transference of many
of his ironic techniques and makes the critic's task of tracing the
development of his techniques from genre to genre difficult at best.
After all, if the verbal irony of *Joseph Andrews* is ultimately more
effective than that of *The Champion* – as it clearly is – it is only
because the different requirements of the novel provided him with
a form that was more congenial to a mode that could, ideally,
transform style as well as govern satiric method. This would ob-

[9]   See, for example, *Jonathan Wild*, pp. 99, 102, 106-7, 124, 137, and 159.

viously account for Fielding's use of connotative irony in the two
novels – particularly in *Joseph Andrews* – and not elsewhere in his
early works.

However, aside from the connection that I have already discussed between Medley's self-conscious (and non-ironic) intrusion
in *The Historical Register*, and the ironic manipulation by the self-
conscious, ironic narrator in *Joseph Andrews* of both narrative and
reader, there *is* one important link between two widely separated
techniques – situational ambiguity and connotative irony. Each of
these techniques relies for its ironic effects on fundamental ambiguities of either situation or character, suggesting that the one
may be considered an extension of the other. More specifically, the
similarity of method suggests that connotative irony is a stylistic
analogue to a more broadly applied dramatic technique – an analogue in which a series of verbal variants create different sets of
verbal ambiguities. Despite Fielding's awareness and possible imitation of Swift's use of connotative irony, it is possible, then, to
claim a degree of continuity between Fielding the ironic dramatist
and Fielding the ironic novelist, particularly since the techniques
involved are so central to the ironic impact of the works in which
he employs them.

The final problem of development of ironic techniques involves
the relationship of the irony of the two novels of this early period.
As we move from *Joseph Andrews* to *Jonathan Wild*, what is immediately apparent about Fielding's adaptation of the infamous
criminal's biography is the relative lack of subtlety of its irony, for
aside from his only occasional use of connotative irony, Fielding
relies most heavily in *Jonathan Wild* on the most transparent of
verbal devices to achieve his ironic effects. Characteristic of his
method in this novel is his constant repetition of terms that require
the reader to make a simple denotative reversal. Whenever Fielding says "great" (or "greatness"), he really means "mean" (or
"meanness"); and when he says "hero", he really means "villain".[10]

---

[10]   See Fielding's definition of "great" in his "Modern Glossary": "applied
to a thing, signifies bigness; when to a man, often littleness or meanness."
In his Preface to the 1743 *Miscellanies*, he further associates greatness
with villainy. (*Works* [Henley], XII, pp. 244-6.)

Part of the effect also stems from the concentration or massing of ironic words or statements in a limited space and not from the subtle rapier thrusts that give *Joseph Andrews* its stylistic lightness and brilliance.

What is perhaps an even better indication of the relative weakness of the irony in *Jonathan Wild* is Fielding's failure to utilize fully his verbal techniques in situations where their effect could have been devastating. Nowhere is this more effectively illustrated than in the contrast between the introductory characterizations in *Jonathan Wild* and those in *Joseph Andrews*. Compare, for example, Fielding's initial descriptions of Tom Smirk and Fireblood in *Jonathan Wild* with that of Beau Didapper. First, Tom Smirk, the London beau:

> Mr. *Wild* was no sooner departed, than the fair Conqueress, opening the Door of a Closet, called forth a young Gentleman, whom she had there enclosed at the Approach of the other. The Name of this Gallant was *Tom Smirk*. He was an Apprentice to a Tallow-Chandler, and was indeed the greatest Beau, and the greatest Favourite of the Ladies, at the End of the Town when he lived. As we take Dress to be the Characteristic or efficient Quality of a Beau, we shall, instead of giving any Character of this young Gentleman, content ourselves with describing his Dress only to our Readers. He wore, then, a Pair of white Stockings on his Legs, and Pumps on his Feet; his Buckles were a large Piece of *Pinchbeck* Plate, which almost covered his whole Foot. His Breeches were of red Plush, which hardly reached his Knees; his Wastecoat was a white Dimity richly embroidered with yellow Silk, over which he wore a blue plush Coat with Metal Buttons, a smart Sleeve, and a Cape reaching half way down his Back. His Wig was of a brown Colour, covering almost half his Pate, on which was hung on one side a little laced Hat, but cocked with great Smartness. Such was the accomplished *Smirk*, who, at his issuing forth from the Closet, was received with open Arms by the amiable *Laetitia*.[11]

Then Fireblood, "the most promising" of Wild's gang, and introduced, as was Didapper, in wholly "negative" terms:

> The Name of this Youth, who will hereafter make some Figure in this History, being the *Achates* of our *Aeneas*, or rather the *Haephestion*

[11]   Pp. 43-4 (I, x).

of our *Alexander* was *Fireblood*. He had every Qualification to make a Second-Rate GREAT MAN; or in other Words, he was completely equipped for the Tool of a Real or First-Rate GREAT MAN. We shall therefore (which is the properest Way of dealing with this Kind of GREATNESS) describe him negatively, and content ourselves with telling our Reader what Qualities he had not: In which Number were Humanity, Modesty, and Fear, not one Grain of any of which was mingled in his whole Composition.[12]

Now, compare these to Fielding's introduction to Didapper, who is also, as it turns out, dependent on the good will of a "great man".

Mr. Didapper, or beau Didapper, was a young gentleman of about four foot five inches in height. He wore his own hair, though the scarcity of it might have given him sufficient excuse for a periwig. His face was thin and pale; the shape of his body and legs none of the best, for he had very narrow shoulders, and no calf; and his gait might more properly be called hopping than walking. The qualifications of his mind were well adapted to his person. We shall handle them first negatively. He was not entirely ignorant; for he could talk a little French, and sing two or three Italian songs: he had lived too much in the world to be bashful, and too much at court to be proud: he seemed not much inclined to avarice; for he was profuse in his expenses: nor had he all the features of prodigality; for he never gave a shilling: no hater of women; for he always dangled after them; yet so little subject to lust, that he had, among those who knew him best, the character of great moderation in his pleasures. No drinker of wine; nor so addicted to passion but that a hot word or two from an adversary made him immediately cool.

Now, to give him only a dash or two on the affirmative side: though he was born to an immense fortune, he chose, for the pitiful and dirty consideration of a place of little consequence, to depend entirely on the will of a fellow, whom they call a great man; who treated him with the utmost disrespect, and exacted of him a plenary obedience to his commands; which he implicitly submitted to, at the expense of his conscience, his honour, and of his country, in which he had himself so large a share. And to finish his character; as he was entirely well satisfied with his own person and parts, so he was very apt to ridicule and laugh at any imperfection in another. Such was the little person, or rather thing, that hopped after Lady Booby into Mr. Adam's kitchen.[13]

[12] P. 135 (III, iv).
[13] Pp. 311-12 (IV, ix).

In *Jonathan Wild* – in compelling contrast to his manner in *Joseph Andrews* – Fielding seemed almost fearful that a reader would mistake his irony. Again and again he employs the most explicit devices to insure the correct response to his ridicule. A case in point is his use of "chaste" with Laetitia. In *Joseph Andrews*, as I have already pointed out, the word had subtle, connotatively ironic overtones when applied to Slipslop, but in *Jonathan Wild* the word is denotatively false: from the beginning of the novel, Laetitia is clearly unchaste, in fact, promiscuous. Yet on two occasions Fielding takes the trouble to parenthetically draw the reader's attention to the word in the most obvious manner, a practice he never follows in *Joseph Andrews*.

How must our Reader, who perhaps had wisely accounted for the Resistance which the chaste *Laetitia* had made to the violent Addresses of the ravished (or rather ravishing) *Wild* from that Lady's impregnable Virtue, how must he blush, I say, to perceive her quit the Strictness of her Carriage, and abandon herself to those loose Freedoms which she indulged to *Smirk*. But, alas! when we discover all, as, to preserve the Fidelity of our History, we must, when we relate that every Familiarity had passed between them, and that the FAIR *Laetitia* (for we must, in this single Instance, imitate *Virgil*, where he drops the *pius* and the *pater*, and drop our favourite Epithet of *chaste*) the FAIR *Laetitia* had, I say, made *Smirk* as happy as Wild desired to be, what must then be our Reader's Confusion?

And much later in the novel:

Mr. *Wild* and his Lady were at Breakfast, when Mr. *Snap*, with all the Agonies of Despair both in his Voice and Countenance, brought them this melancholy News. Our Hero, who had (as we have said) wonderful Good-Nature when his GREATNESS or Interest was not concerned, instead of reviling his Sister-in-law, asked with a Smile: "Who was the Father?" But the chaste *Laetitia*, we repeat *the chaste,* for well did she now deserve that Epithet, received it in another Manner.[14]

Then too, Fielding's use of the ironic foil in *Jonathan Wild* is based for the most part on fairly superficial contrasts. At the beginning of the second book, Fielding takes the trouble to explain to the reader that he is deliberately opposing Heartfree to Wild:

[14] P. 45 (I, x), and pp. 172-3 (III, xiii).

As our Reader is to be more acquainted with this Person, it may not
be improper to open somewhat of his Character, especially as it will
serve as a Kind of Foil to the noble and GREAT Disposition of our
Hero, and as the one seems sent into this World as a proper Object
on which the GREAT Talents of the other were to be displayed with
a proper and just Success.[15]

Yet, unlike Fielding's practice in *Joseph Andrews*, the verbal irony
here does not establish any underlying ironic tensions between
characters, for the terms of reference are not interchangeable:
Heartfree is "weak, silly, low" – a "poor wretch"; Fielding's "hero",
on the other hand, is "great, illustrious, noble" – a man possessing
"vast abilities". The latter are qualities associated with a man of
traditionally heroic dimension, not with a person like Heartfree,
who is simply a virtuous shopkeeper of humble origins and modest
ability who is forced into unequal conflict with villainy.

Finally, it should be noted that in *Jonathan Wild* occurs Fielding's only extensive use of praise-by-blame (as denotative irony) in
his early works. Considering the popularity of this technique in the
early eighteenth century, it is surprising to note how infrequently
Fielding uses it. The satires of Swift and the other Scriblerians
must certainly have made him conscious of its effectiveness. Yet,
he was probably also aware of the danger that was more inherent
in praise-by-blame then in any other ironic technique: to blame by
praising involves no real risks, for if the person whom the ironist
praises does not perceive the irony, nothing is lost; indeed, the person's obtuseness may even increase the pleasure of those who are
in on the joke. But if the ironist praises a friend by blaming him
and the friend fails to perceive the irony, the loss then becomes
prohibitive. That Fielding was aware of how easily irony could be
misunderstood has been noted above.[16] Significantly, in *Jonathan
Wild* Fielding praises by blaming only when he is describing fictional characters so obviously praiseworthy that there is no possibility
of mistaking his intention. His caution here, as well as that noted
elsewhere in *Jonathan Wild*, the relative lack of subtlety, the rather
unsophisticated manner of achieving his ironic effects all tend to

[15]   P. 67 (II, i).
[16]   See Chapter I, p. 30.

diminish the novel's importance as a vehicle for irony. And this, if such an inference can be drawn from internal evidence based upon the quality of the novel's irony, seems in turn to provide additional proof for Professor McKillop's contention [17] that *Jonathan Wild* was, in large part, written considerably earlier than *Joseph Andrews* and put aside until Fielding decided to include it in the 1743 *Miscellanies*. There is otherwise no satisfactory explanation for his failure to utilize the techniques he learned while writing *Joseph Andrews*.

If *Joseph Andrews*, by virtue of its verbal irony alone, achieves a clear superiority over *Jonathan Wild*, it also must be regarded as the high point in Fielding's use of irony in his early works as a whole, for, however functional the dramatic irony of the plays and the two forms of rhetorical irony (the *persona* and verbal irony) in *The Champion*, it was in *Joseph Andrews* that Fielding's development as an ironist came to fruition. Any judgment of the formal or aesthetic values of this novel must, then, be made with some awareness of the effectiveness of Fielding's irony generally and of his verbal techniques in particular.

It was not until *Joseph Andrews* that Fielding became fully aware of the comic, satiric, and structural potential of irony as a literary device. But it is apparent too that in *Joseph Andrews* irony came to be more than a comic, satiric, or structural device, but a mode integral to the very style itself of the novel – something he was never able to accomplish in his other early works. In this lies the achievement of this novel – an achievement that was lead to an even greater triumph several years later in the intricate and constantly shifting ironies that informed the mood, the tone, and the structure of *Tom Jones*.

[17]   A. D. McKillop, *The Early Masters of English Fiction* (Lawrence, Kansas, 1956), p. 117.

A NOTE ON THE TEXTS CITED

I have used the Henley edition of Fielding's works throughout (*The Complete Works of Henry Fielding, Esq.*, ed. W. E. Henley, 16 vols., New York, 1902), except where I have quoted from works not in Henley and where textually better editions exist.

For those *Champion* essays not in Henley, I have used the 1741 reprinting of the more complete collection of the essays (*The Champion: Containing a Series of Papers, Humorous, Moral, Political, and Critical*, 2 vols., London, 1741), and the Augustan Reprint Society's edition of the Job Vinegar papers (*The Voyages of Mr. Job Vinegar*, ed. with an Introduction by S. J. Sackett, Los Angeles, 1958).

When quoting from the *Covent-Garden Journal*, I have used the edition of Gerard E. Jensen, 2 vols. (New Haven, 1915).

For *Joseph Andrews*, I have used the 1742 second edition (published August, 1742), reprinted in Maynard Mack's Rinehart edition (New York, 1948) which I have compared with J. Paul de Castro's edition (London, 1929).

And for *Jonathan Wild*, I have used the "Oxford World's Classics" reprinting (London, 1951) of the 1743 edition as it first appeared in Fielding's *Miscellanies*.

INDEX

Paulson, Ronald, 24n
"Philalethes", 31n
Plumb, John H., 35n
Pope, Alexander, 16, 21, 23n, 25, 38, 39, 65, 70, 78, 79n, 81, 89; *Dunciad*, 39; *Dunciad Variorum*, 33, 42; *Essay on Criticism*, 38, 39; "Of the Characters of Women", 95; *Peribathous*, 33, 39
Price, Martin, 21n, 22, 23, 72
"prudence" in *Joseph Andrews*, 94-6
Pulteney, William, 47, 48n
Puttenham, George, 7

Quintana, Ricardo, 143n

raillery, 14, 18, 19, 29, 30
Ralph, James, 31n, 35, 55
Rand, Benjamin, 17n
Redinger, Ruby, 23n
Rich, John, 146
Richardson, Samuel, 136, 150; *Pamela*, 42, 100, 118, 148, 149
Ross, John H., 19n

Sackett, S. J., 55n
"Scriblerus Secundus", 33, 37-42
Sedgewick, G. G., 11n, 12n, 126n
Shaftesbury, Anthony Ashley Cooper, Earl of, 17
Smith, D. Nichol, 17n
Socrates, 11, 17, 20
Spectator, The, 31, 147
Speer, John F., 35n, 55n
Spilka, Mark, 100n
Steele, Sir Richard, 31, 147

Swift, Jonathan, 15-17, 19n, 21, 22, 25, 32, 62-4, 65, 72, 73, 81, 82n, 83, 151, 155; *Argument Against Abolishing Christianity*, 24, 63; *Drapier's Letters*, 63; *Gulliver's Travels*, 22, 23, 32, 42, 56, 60, 61, 63, 94n; *Modest Proposal*, 22, 31, 50, 63, 64; "Some Advice . . . to Members of the October Club", 22-3; *Tale of a Tub*, 15, 16, 24, 57, 62-3; *Vindication of . . . Lord C[artere]t*, 23

Tatler, The, 38n, 147
Thirlwall, Bishop Connop, 12n
Thompson, A. R., 126n
Thomson, J. A. K., 11n, 20
"Trottplaid, John, Esq.", 30

"Vinegar, Captain, Hercules", 31, 35, 55, 56
"Vinegar, Mr. Job", 32, 55-62

Wagstaffe, William, 40n
Walpole, Sir Robert, 31n, 34, 35, 35n, 36, 43, 44, 45, 46, 48n, 50, 51, 53-4, 55, 141, 146
Warren, Austin, 25n
Watt, Ian, 16n, 21n
Wharton, Thomas, 1st Earl, 81-2n
White, E. B., 7
Williams, Basil, 45n
Williams, Harold, 15n
Wimsatt, W. K., 25n
Worcester, David, 16, 126n

Young, The Reverend William, 26n